WINTER TREE IDENTIFICATION

FOR THE SOUTHERN APPALACHIANS AND PIEDMONT

A PHOTOGRAPHIC GUIDE

DONALD L. HAGAN · CRYSTAL STRICKLAND · HAILEY MALONE

Terminal bud of sugar maple (Acer saccharum)

WINTER TREE IDENTIFICATION

FOR THE SOUTHERN APPALACHIANS AND PIEDMONT

A PHOTOGRAPHIC GUIDE

DONALD L. HAGAN · CRYSTAL STRICKLAND · HAILEY MALONE

CLEMSON
UNIVERSITY
PRESS

ISBN 978-1-949979-14-5

Published by Clemson University Press in Clemson, South Carolina

Designed by Richard Jividen, TEN2design

This book is set in Adobe Caslon Pro.

To order copies, visit our website: www.clemson.edu/press.

PROLOGUE

For a dendrology student or novice plant enthusiast, there are few things more intimidating than winter tree identification. After all, trees are difficult enough to identify during the rest of the year. Just imagine how difficult they must be when one of their most obvious features, the foliage, has fallen off. The tremendous diversity of deciduous tree species in the southern Appalachians and Piedmont increases the anxiety factor even more. As a dendrology professor at Clemson University, I see this trepidation every year, usually around November. I tell the students that it's not hard; just grab a twig, focus on this feature, and then that one—and they'll be identifying leafless trees in no time. Some students believe me, whereas others are convinced that it is a special kind of torture.

THERE HAS TO BE A BETTER WAY.

There are several excellent resources for winter tree identification. However, existing books are largely geared toward a very taxonomically literate audience, with heavy reliance on specialized terminology and complex dichotomous keys. They often have few illustrations or photos. Recognizing the dearth of novice-friendly winter tree identification resources and wishing to update the teaching materials for my dendrology class, I decided in 2016 to buy a camera and create a study guide for my students. But there was one problem: I knew nothing about photography. So I enlisted the help of a talented photographer (and Clemson undergraduate), Crystal Strickland, to take care of that part. Later, one of Crystal's classmates, Hailey Malone, joined the team—lending her artistic hand to produce diagrams and drawings. After seeing the quality of Crystal's and Hailey's work, I decided that this could be more than just a study guide for my students. It should be a book. And that is how Winter Tree Identification for the Southern Appalachians and Piedmont: A Photographic Guide was born.

The book is designed to be easy to use. The "How to Use This Book, Step by Step" section provides an overview of basic twig morphology and terminology and includes helpful drawings and diagrams. Species are organized by readily observable features—namely, leaf scar orientation and bud characteristics—and then further ordered by family (suffix "-aceae") and then by Latin name within the family. For each species, high-resolution color photographs clearly show the key twig, bark, and fruit features. Leaf pictures are also included, because leaves on the ground can often aid with identification, especially when twigs are difficult to reach. Concise and easy-to-read text highlights the key features shown in each photograph. "Similar species in winter" is provided for each entry to allow for quick comparisons of easily confused species. The "Glossary of Key Terms" at the end provides definitions of common technical terms used in the book. The book design provides plenty of white space to facilitate notetaking in the field. Thus, we encourage you to take this book with you any time you are hiking, exploring, or studying plants in the wintertime.

We hope you enjoy the book!

Dr. Donald L. Hagan
Clemson University

HOW TO USE THIS BOOK, STEP BY STEP

You do not have to be an expert to successfully identify trees in the wintertime. In fact, with a little practice, you'll likely find that you can quickly identify an unknown species in only a few simple steps.

Winter tree identification largely focuses on twigs; so, before you get started, you'll need to familiarize yourself with the basics of twig anatomy (page 1). Although many twigs may look similar at first glance, you'll find that each species has a unique combination of bud, leaf scar, and other characteristics. These features are highly conserved; that is, within a given species, they are reliable and do not vary much, but they differ substantially between species—even those with similar leaves. But beware: Many of these features are small and easy to overlook.

> **STEP 1**—Collect a twig from a tree, preferably more than one. Twig characteristics, particularly color and size, can vary somewhat from sample to sample—even for the same species. So looking at multiple twigs will give you a better appreciation for the full range of variability that a species can have.

> **STEP 2**—Identify the leaf scar arrangement. That is, how many leaf scars are there per node? Are they alternate, opposite, or whorled?[1]

> **STEP 3**—Look at the bud scales. Are they imbricate, naked, valvate, or cap-like buds? Are they clustered at the end of the twig?[1]

> **STEP 4**—Identify the twig. Flip to the appropriate section of the book (twigs are primarily organized by leaf scar arrangement and bud scales), and use the descriptions and photos to identify your unknown twig. Within each section, species are listed alphabetically by family, and then by Latin name within family.

This simple four-step approach can help you identify nearly every tree in the southern Appalachians and Piedmont. However, some species do not neatly fit into leaf scar and bud scale categories. For these species, flip to the last two sections: "Alternate and Stout with a Large Leaf Scar" and "Alternate and Slender with a Small Leaf Scar." Bark, leaf, and fruit characteristics can also aid in identification; for this reason, you will find additional descriptions and photos of "nontwig" features for all species.

---

[1] See "Twig Anatomy: The Basics" for a labeled diagram of a typical twig.
   Alternate = 1, opposite = 2, whorled = 3

CONTENTS

TWIG ANATOMY: THE BASICS

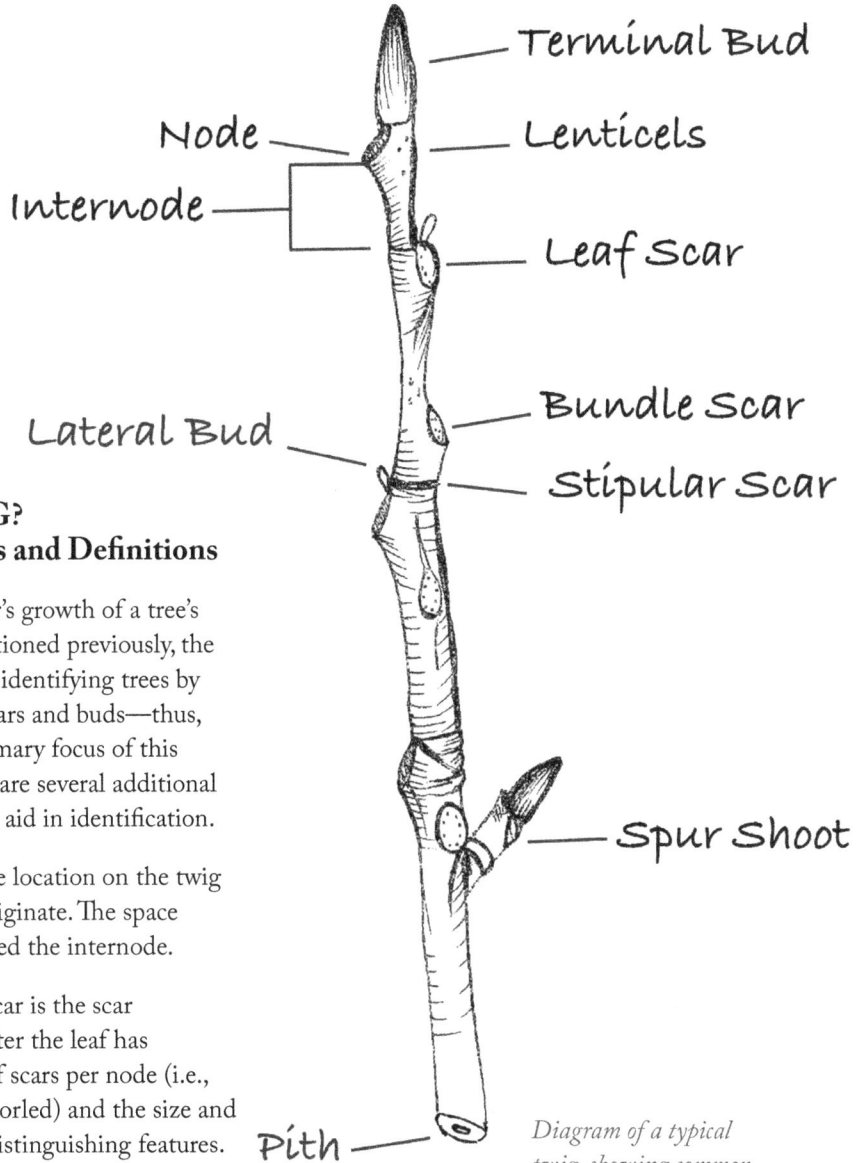

Terminal Bud

Node

Lenticels

Internode

Leaf Scar

Bundle Scar

Lateral Bud

Stipular Scar

Spur Shoot

WHAT IS A TWIG?
Some Basic Features and Definitions

A twig is the current year's growth of a tree's shoot or branch. As mentioned previously, the most reliable features for identifying trees by their twigs are the leaf scars and buds—thus, these features are the primary focus of this book. Nonetheless, there are several additional features of twigs that can aid in identification.

NODE—The node is the location on the twig where leaves and buds originate. The space between the nodes is called the internode.

LEAF SCAR—A leaf scar is the scar remaining on the twig after the leaf has fallen. The number of leaf scars per node (i.e., alternate, opposite, or whorled) and the size and shape of scar(s) are key distinguishing features. Additionally, some leaf scars contain visible bundle scars (scars left from when the vascular tissue was severed during leaf fall), which can also aid in identification.

BUD—A bud is an undeveloped shoot or

Pith

Diagram of a typical twig, showing common features that are useful for identification

flower, often covered with protective scales (see page 4). Terminal buds are found at the end of the twig, whereas lateral buds are found farther down. This book primarily focuses on buds that produce shoots, although some species do have distinctive flower buds in the winter that can aid with identification.

LENTICEL—A lenticel is a raised and sometimes corky pore on the twig that enables gas exchange between the living cells below the bark and the atmosphere.

STIPULAR SCAR—Some trees produce stipules, which are deciduous leaf-like appendages found at the base of the petiole. When a stipule falls off, it can leave a distinctive scar, often encircling the twig.

PITH—The central portion of the twig is called the pith. It can be hollow, solid, spongy, or partitioned into small segments or chambers.

SPUR SHOOT—A spur shoot is a short shoot or twig. Internodes on spur shoots are typically very short, making the leaves or leaf scars appear whorled, even when they are not.

TEXTURE—Some twigs and buds are smooth (glabrous), others shiny (lustrous) or covered by a whitish/waxy coating (glaucous). Distinctive hairs are also present on some species. These hairs can be fine and velvety (pubescent), coarse and wooly (tomentose), or sparse.

ARMAMENT—A few twigs are armed with sharp thorns, prickles, or stipular spines for protection. Readily observable when present, these features can greatly aid with identification.

LEAF SCARS

 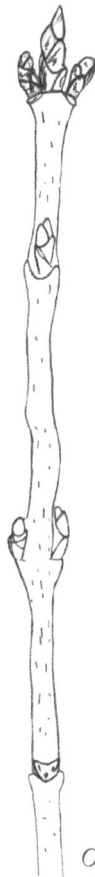 

Alternate = 1   *Opposite = 2*   *Whorled = 3*

ALTERNATE—In an alternate arrangement, each node has one leaf scar and one bud. This is the largest category of twigs and includes several important species groups, including oaks, birches, beeches, elms, and hickories, among others. Note that individual twigs with short internodes may sometimes appear opposite or whorled, when they are in fact alternate.

OPPOSITE—In an opposite arrangement, each node has two leaf scars and two buds. This encompasses the second largest category of twigs, including maples, ashes, and dogwoods.

WHORLED—In a whorled arrangement, each node has three leaf scars and three buds. This is the smallest category of twigs; catalpa is the only common member of this group in the region.

BUD SCALES

Imbricate   valvate   Cap-like   Naked

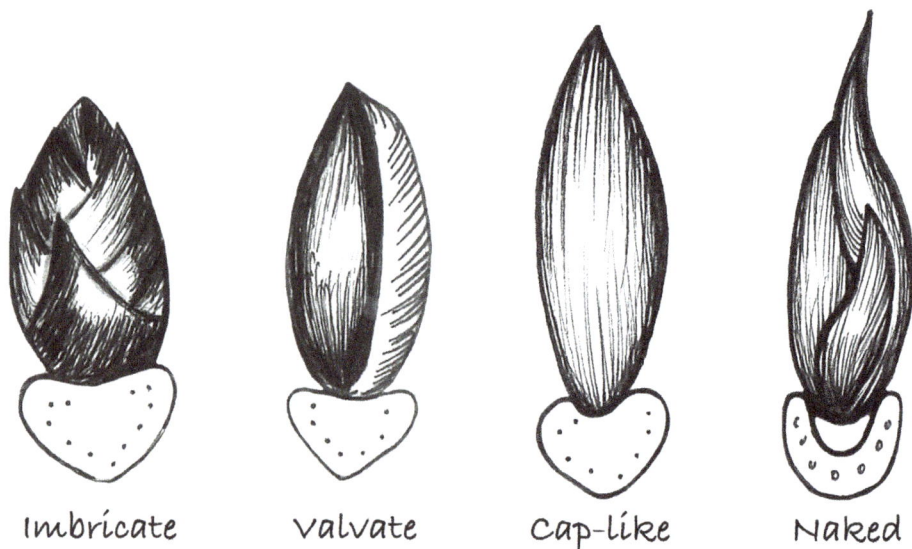

Examples of different bud scale types: imbricate, valvate, cap-like, and naked buds

IMBRICATE—Buds covered with multiple scales, overlapping like shingles on a roof, are called imbricate. This is the most common type of bud, including important species groups like oaks, birches, beeches, and elms, among others.

VALVATE—Buds covered with two nonoverlapping scales, coming together like a clamshell or "praying hands," are called valvate. This bud scale type is characteristic of common species such as yellow-poplars and hazel alders.

CAP-LIKE—Buds covered with a single, usually pointed, scale are called cap-like buds. This bud type is characteristic of common species such as willows and American sycamores.

NAKED—Buds lacking bud scales, often covered with fine pubescence, are called naked. This type is characteristic of common species such as pawpaw, Carolina buckthorn, and witch hazel.

OTHER THINGS TO LOOK FOR

Although twigs are the most reliable feature for winter tree identification, it is often useful—if not necessary—to pay attention to other characteristics. This is especially true for species that look similar in winter, like oaks, some maples, and those with slender twigs and/or small buds. Additionally, on a tall tree, fresh twigs may not be easily accessible. In these cases, focusing on bark, fruit, and senescent (fallen) leaves can be helpful. And it is always good practice to identify species based on a "preponderance of the evidence," taking into consideration all available information. For these reasons, we have included pictures of bark and leaves for all species, as well as fruits for many species that can possess mature fruits in the wintertime.

BARK—Bark is the outermost layer of the stems and roots of woody plants (trees, shrubs, and vines). For many species, bark characteristics such as texture, thickness, and color can greatly aid in identification. However, it is important to remember that bark characteristics will often change as a tree matures. Younger trees, for example, often have smoother, thinner, and lighter colored bark than mature ones. All bark pictures in this book are from mature trees.

A comparison of bark characteristics from a young tree (left) and a mature tree (right)

LEAVES—Leaves, a tree's photosynthetic organs, can be a useful identification feature even after they fall off. Freshly fallen leaves, though lacking the color they had in the spring and summer, often retain their original shape and texture for a few months. Some species (e.g., American beech) are tardily deciduous, meaning that they retain some of their senesced leaves well into the winter. Fallen leaves, however, often present challenges when they are mixed with the leaves of other species.

FRUITS—Fruits are seed-bearing organs, borne from the female reproductive structures (flowers) of angiosperm trees. There are many different types of fruits, such as nuts (including acorns), legumes, capsules, and samaras. Some of these fruits are unique and/or conspicuous and present in the wintertime—either still attached to the tree or freshly fallen on the ground. Thus, they can sometimes be useful as identification aids, particularly for mature trees. Like leaves, however, fallen fruits can sometimes be problematic in cases where it is difficult to determine the tree of origin.

GENERAL KEY

GROUP 1

OPPOSITE OR WHORLED LEAF SCARS

FLORIDA MAPLE

Sapindaceae
Acer barbatum

GENERAL DESCRIPTION

A small- to medium-sized tree, occasionally to 60 feet tall, often with a short trunk and elliptical crown. Typically an understory species in fertile, mesic sites in the Piedmont and Coastal Plain, often along streams. Generally not found in the mountains. Simple and opposite leaves are up to 4 inches across, with three to five palmate lobes and rounded sinuses. Most features of Florida maple are very similar to those of sugar maple, only smaller.

WINTER ID FEATURES

Twig and leaf scars: Lustrous and reddish-brown, with light-colored lenticels. Similar to sugar maple, but thinner. Leaf scars opposite and V-shaped, as with all maples. Apices of the two V-shaped leaf scars touch, or nearly do. Small, circular bundle scars within the leaf scar may be visible with a hand lens.

Buds: Terminal buds are pointed, with distinctively imbricate brown bud scales. Lateral buds appressed to the twig, and smaller than terminals. Unlike sugar maple, bud scales on the Florida maple are typically pubescent.

Bark: Similar to sugar maple.

Fruits: A samara, similar to sugar maple, but smaller.

Similar species in winter: Sugar maple (18).

BOXELDER

Sapindaceae
Acer negundo

GENERAL DESCRIPTION

A fast-growing tree, up to 70 feet tall, with an irregularly shaped crown. Most commonly found in floodplains, bottomlands, and other moist sites in both the Piedmont and mountains. Pinnately compound leaves, containing three to seven leaflets, distinguish it in the summer from other maples that have simple leaves.

WINTER ID FEATURES

Twig and leaf scars: Glabrous or lustrous, usually green, sometimes purple or reddish-brown. Leaf scars opposite and V-shaped, as with all maples. Apices of the two V-shaped leaf scars touch, or nearly do. Small circular bundle scars within the leaf scar may be visible with a hand lens.

Buds: Imbricate bud scales covered with a dense, cottony pubescence.

Bark: Grayish-brown, developing shallow fissures with age. Epicormic branches common.

Fruits: Paired green samaras, maturing in the summer, then turning brown. Generally not present on the tree in winter, but may be visible on the ground.

Similar species in winter: Flowering dogwood (page 26).

STRIPED MAPLE

Sapindaceae
Acer pensylvanicum

GENERAL DESCRIPTION

A small, shrubby maple, occasionally up to 40 feet tall, found primarily in mid- to high-elevation mountains in the southern Appalachians. Generally found on moist upland soils, typically below other deciduous hardwoods. Leaves are simple and opposite, with three lobes, a rounded or heart-shaped base, and rugose (sunken) veins.

WINTER ID FEATURES

Twig and leaf scars: Stout and glabrous, with color ranging from green to black, or green/black stripes. Leaf scars opposite and V-shaped, as with all maples. Apices of the two V-shaped leaf scars touch, or nearly do. Small circular bundle scars within the leaf scar may be visible with a hand lens.

Buds: Two glabrous bud scales, giving it a valvate appearance. Lateral buds are stalked and substantially smaller than terminals.

Bark: Green, tending toward black with age. Stripes often present.

Fruits: Paired samaras, maturing in the early fall. Wings are widely divergent. Often not present in the winter due to herbivory.

Similar species in winter: Mountain maple (page 20).

RED MAPLE

Sapindaceae
Acer rubrum

GENERAL DESCRIPTION

Often a large tree, up to 90 feet tall, red maple is one of the largest and most common maples in the southern Appalachian and Piedmont regions. Found on a range of sites, from dry uplands to wetlands. Leaves are simple and opposite. Leaf morphology can be highly variable; some leaves have distinct pointed lobes, others are nearly unlobed. Petioles are generally red. Undersides of the leaves are usually silvery or whitish.

WINTER ID FEATURES

Twig and leaf scars: Slender and red or reddish-brown. Leaf scars opposite and V-shaped, as with all maples. Apices of the two V-shaped leaf scars touch, or nearly do. Small circular bundle scars within the leaf scar may be visible with a hand lens.

Buds: Imbricate bud scales; terminal generally larger than laterals. Globose flower buds sometimes present on each side of lateral buds.

Bark: Smooth and gray on young trees; narrow scaly plates developing with age.

Fruits: Paired red or reddish-brown samaras, maturing in the spring.

Similar species in winter: Silver maple (page 16).

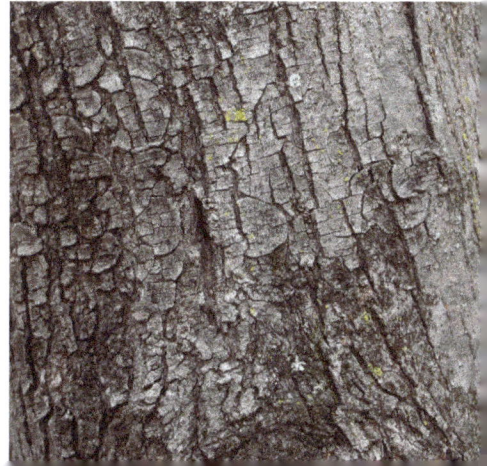

SILVER MAPLE

Sapindaceae
Acer saccharinum

GENERAL DESCRIPTION

Often a large tree, up to 80 feet tall, typically with a short trunk that forks into several large, spreading branches. Not common in the region, aside from landscape plantings. Occurs occasionally in floodplains, along streambanks and other poorly drained mesic areas. Leaves are simple and opposite, with five deeply incised lobes. The underside of the leaf has a distinctive silver color. Petioles are often red, similar to red maple.

WINTER ID FEATURES

Twig and leaf scars: Slender and dark red, sometimes brownish, similar to red maple. Unlike red maple, has a disagreeable odor when crushed or cut. Leaf scars opposite and V-shaped, as with all maples. Apices of the two V-shaped leaf scars touch, or nearly do. Small circular bundle scars within the leaf scar may be visible with a hand lens.

Buds: Terminal bud is large, dark red and lustrous, similar to red maple. Globose flower buds sometimes present near laterals.

Bark: Smooth and gray when young, becoming darker gray and scaly, sometimes flaky, on larger trees.

Fruits: A large (2- to 3-inch) tan or yellowish-brown paired samara. Unlike other maples, one seed typically aborts during early development, such that mature fruits often have only one wing.

Similar species in winter: Red maple (page 14).

SUGAR MAPLE

Sapindaceae
Acer saccharum

GENERAL DESCRIPTION

A medium- to large-sized tree (up to 80 feet tall), commonly found in fertile moist slopes in the southern Appalachians, particularly in northern hardwood plant communities. It is sporadic in the Piedmont, occasionally occurring on protected mesic slopes. Leaves are simple and opposite, with distinctive five-lobed leaves that are similar to Florida maple but larger.

WINTER ID FEATURES

Twig and leaf scars: Lustrous and reddish brown, with light-colored lenticels. Leaf scars opposite and V-shaped, as with all maples. Apices of the two V-shaped leaf scars touch, or nearly do. Small circular bundle scars within the leaf scar may be visible with a hand lens.

Buds: Terminal buds are pointed, with distinctively imbricate bud scales. Lateral buds appressed to the twig, and smaller than terminals.

Bark: Thin and gray with shallow fissures on young trees. Bark becomes darker and more deeply furrowed with age.

Fruits: Paired samaras, produced in clusters, maturing in the early fall. Wings are nearly parallel.

Similar species in winter: Florida maple (page 8).

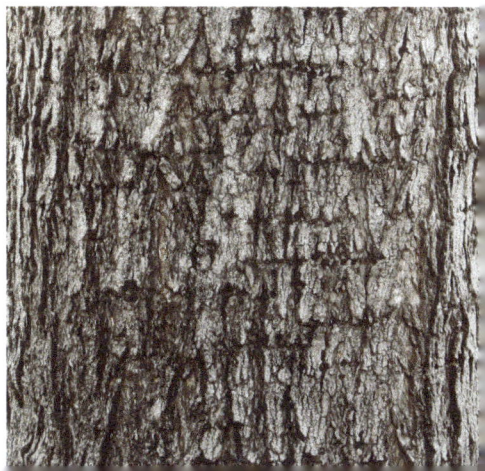

MOUNTAIN MAPLE

Sapindaceae
Acer spicatum

GENERAL DESCRIPTION

A shrub or small tree, typically under 30 feet tall, found sporadically above 4,500 feet in the southern Appalachians. Often associated with northern hardwood and spruce–fir plant communities. Leaves are simple and opposite with variable morphology, much like red maple, but lacking the silvery/whitish underside. Distinctly rugose (sunken) veins on leaves.

WINTER ID FEATURES

Twig and leaf scars: Slender and pubescent (in contrast with stout glabrous twig of striped maple). Often reddish or pinkish in appearance. Leaf scars opposite and V-shaped, as with all maples. Apices of the two V-shaped leaf scars touch, or nearly do. Small circular bundle scars within the leaf scar may be visible with a hand lens.

Buds: Tiny pubescent reddish-brown buds with two scales, appearing valvate. Stalked lateral buds.

Bark: Reddish-brown and smooth, becoming scaly with age. Often covered with lichens and mosses.

Fruits: Paired samaras, maturing in the early fall. Wings are widely divergent. Often not present in the winter due to herbivory.

Similar species in winter: Striped maple (page 12).

SOUTHERN CATALPA

Bignoniaceae
Catalpa bignonioides

GENERAL DESCRIPTION

A small- to medium-sized tree, occasionally taller than 60 feet. It is often poorly formed, with a short trunk and several stout branches. Typically found on moist soil along streams or open areas. Occasionally planted as an ornamental tree. Occasional in the Piedmont, not found in the mountains unless planted. Large, heart-shaped leaves are simple and usually whorled, but sometimes opposite or alternate.

WINTER ID FEATURES

Twig and leaf scars: Stout and brittle, grayish-brown in color, with a foul odor when freshly crushed. Leaf scars are circular and concave, with abundant bundle scars visible.

Buds: Terminal buds are absent. Lateral buds are small, round, and located above the circular leaf scars.

Bark: Smooth and gray on young trees, becoming grayish-brown and somewhat scaly with age.

Fruits: A unique, cigar-shaped elongated capsule (up to 18 inches long) that splits to release large numbers of flat-winged, feathery seeds. Fruits persist through the winter and can be an excellent feature for identification.

Similar species in winter: Princesstree (page 34).

RUSTY BLACKHAW

Caprifoliaceae
Viburnum rufidulum

GENERAL DESCRIPTION

A shrub or small tree, rarely more than 20 feet tall. Large, spreading branches. Found in the understory across a range of sites, including xeric uplands, mesic lower slopes, and forest edges and roadsides. Infrequent in the mountains. Leaves are simple and opposite, lustrous and dark green on top, lighter green on the bottom. Fine teeth present on the margin. Underside of the leaf and the petioles often have patches of rusty pubescence.

WINTER ID FEATURES

Twig and leaf scars: Slender and gray, typically smooth, sometimes with a reddish-brown color. U-shaped opposite leaf scars.

Buds: Terminal bud is pointed with rusty pubescence covering two valvate scales. Lateral buds similar, but more rounded and smaller.

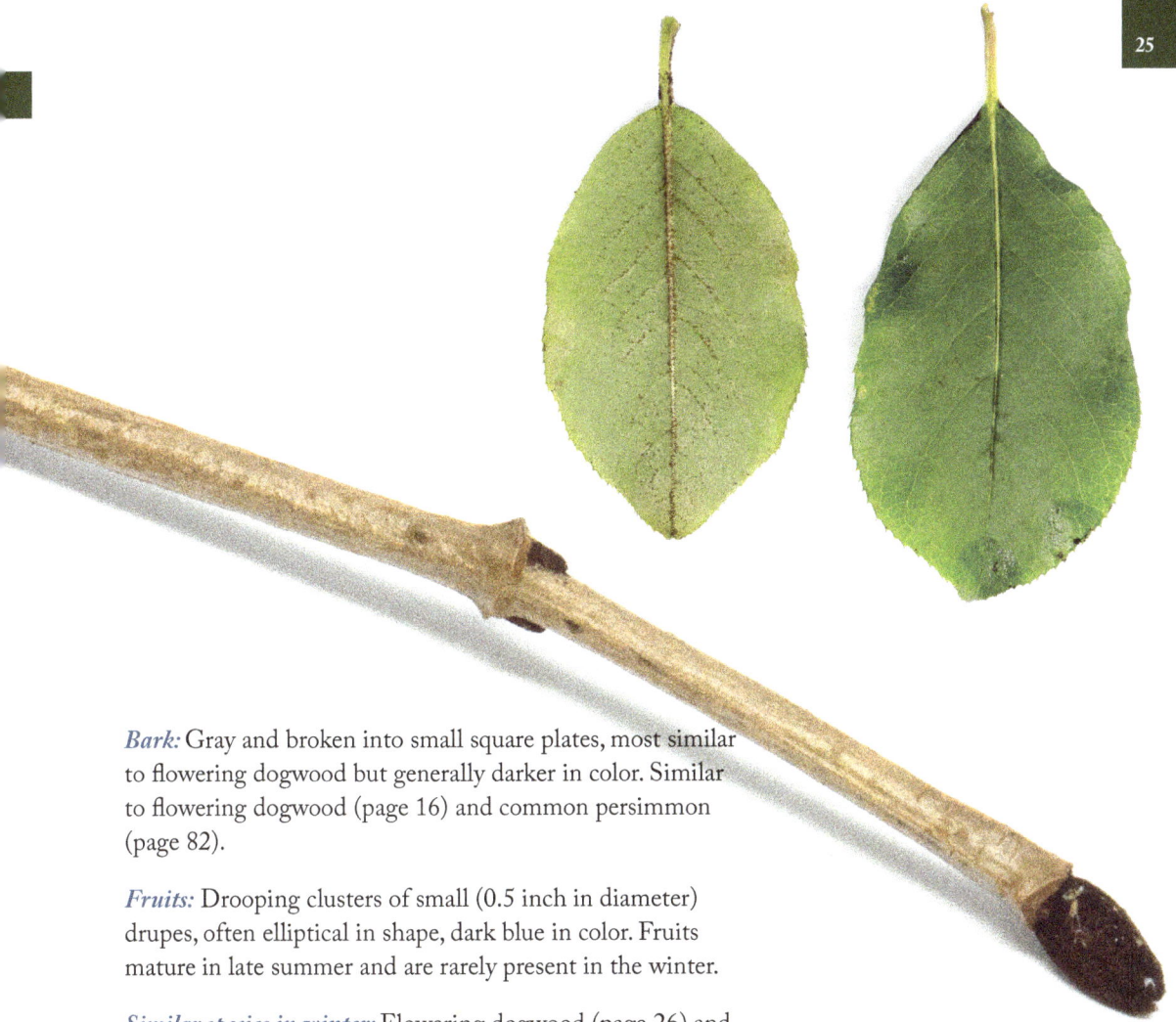

Bark: Gray and broken into small square plates, most similar to flowering dogwood but generally darker in color. Similar to flowering dogwood (page 16) and common persimmon (page 82).

Fruits: Drooping clusters of small (0.5 inch in diameter) drupes, often elliptical in shape, dark blue in color. Fruits mature in late summer and are rarely present in the winter.

Similar species in winter: Flowering dogwood (page 26) and common persimmon (page 160).

FLOWERING DOGWOOD

Cornaceae
Cornus florida

GENERAL DESCRIPTION

Usually a small tree, rarely more than 30 feet tall, often with a short trunk and broad-spreading, upturned branches. An understory/midstory tree found in a range of sites, from well-drained uplands to mesic lower slopes. A common landscape planting. Leaves are simple and opposite, with ovate/elliptical leaves and distinctive arcuate (curved) venation.

WINTER ID FEATURES

Twig and leaf scars: Slender and dull green, becoming purplish later in the winter. Thin leaf scars are opposite nearly encircling the twig. Three small bundle scars visible with a hand lens. Globose flower buds sometimes present in large numbers, especially on trees exposed to full sun.

Buds: Terminal bud is pointed, sometimes hooked, with two valvate scales. Bud emerges from a split at the end of the twig. Lateral buds nearly invisible, hidden within leaf scar.

Bark: Gray and broken into small square or rectangular plates. Similar to rusty blackhaw and common persimmon

Fruits: A small (less than 0.5 inch in diameter), lustrous red drupe, maturing in the fall. Readily consumed by wildlife and, therefore, often not present in the winter.

Similar species in winter: Boxelder (page 10), rusty blackhaw (page 24), and common persimmon (page 160).

YELLOW BUCKEYE

Hippocastanaceae
Aesculus flava

GENERAL DESCRIPTION

Often a large tree, up to 90 feet tall and 3 feet in diameter, with an attractive symmetrical crown. Largely restricted to mesic sites, stream banks, and coves in the mountains. Also found on ridges in areas that receive abundant rainfall. Rare in the Piedmont. Palmately compound, opposite leaves, with five to seven leaflets. One of the first deciduous hardwoods to lose its leaves in the fall.

WINTER ID FEATURES

Twig and leaf scars: Stout and grayish-brown, with prominent lenticels. Large, triangular leaf scars containing up to seven bundle scars. Bundle scars arranged in a distinctive V shape.

Buds: Large (more than 0.5 inch), pointed terminal bud with rounded imbricate bud scales.

Bark: Grayish-brown and smooth when young, becoming darker with flattened exfoliating plates with age. Often covered with lichens and mosses due to the moist habitat.

Fruits: A round, leathery capsule containing up to two lustrous chestnut brown seeds. Seeds are often abundant on the ground in the winter, making them an effective identification aid.

Similar species in winter: None.

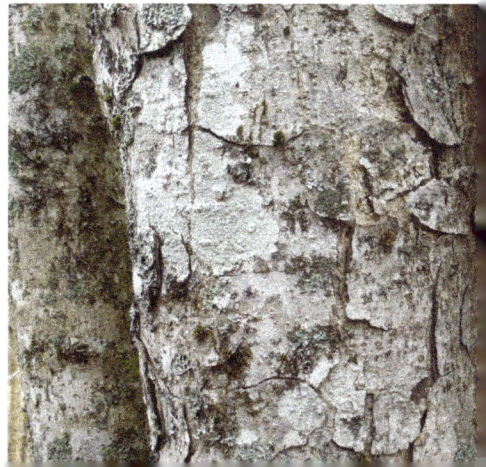

WHITE ASH

Oleaceae
Fraxinus americana

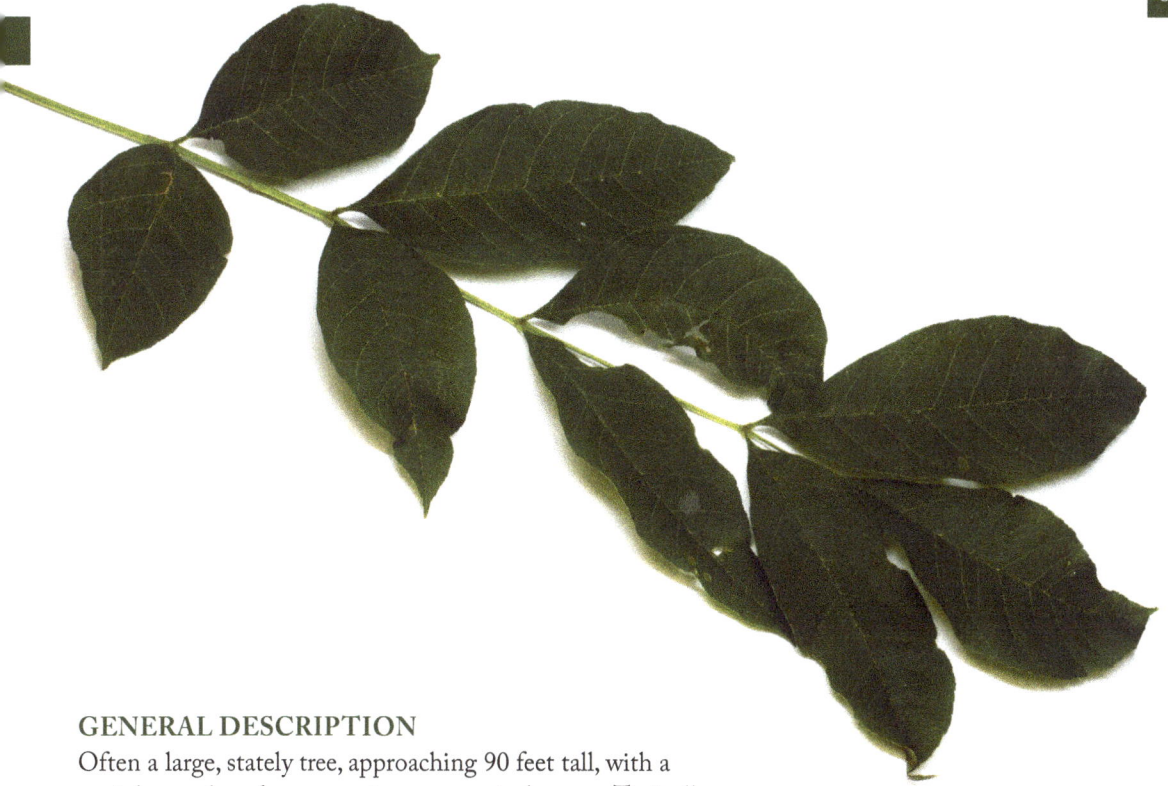

GENERAL DESCRIPTION

Often a large, stately tree, approaching 90 feet tall, with a straight trunk and an attractive symmetrical crown. Typically found on well-drained upland soils, both in the Piedmont and mountains, in contrast with green ash, which is found in wetter sites in the Piedmont. Leaves are pinnately compound and opposite, typically with seven leaflets (occasionally five or nine), dark green on top, lighter green on the bottom.

WINTER ID FEATURES

Twig and leaf scars: Stout and grayish-brown, circular in cross-section, slightly flattened at nodes. Prominent large, light-colored lenticels. Hollow pith. Opposite leaf scars are crescent or U shaped and partially surround the lateral bud.

Buds: Terminal bud is rounded, dark brown or black, with four to eight imbricate bud scales. Lateral buds similar, but smaller.

Bark: Smooth and gray on young trees, becoming fissured with interlacing ridges—similar to some hickories or black walnut—with age. Also similar to green ash, but lighter colored.

Fruits: Single-winged yellowish-brown samaras, generally less than 2 inches long, borne in drooping clusters. Very similar to green ash, except the samara wing does not wrap partially around the seed.

Similar species in winter: Green ash (page 32).

GREEN ASH

Oleaceae
Fraxinus pennsylvanica

GENERAL DESCRIPTION

Often a large tree, approaching 100 feet tall, but with a poorer form than white ash. Typically found on poorly drained floodplain soils and mesic lower slopes. Can tolerate long periods of inundation. Occasionally found on drier sites. Much more common in the Piedmont than the mountains. Leaves are pinnately compound and opposite, typically with seven leaflets (occasionally five or nine), dark green on top, lighter green on the bottom. Winged rachillas (leaflet stalks) distinguish leaves from those of white ash.

WINTER ID FEATURES

Twig and leaf scars: Stout and grayish-green or greenish, circular in cross-section, slightly flattened at nodes. Prominent large, light-colored lenticels. Hollow pith. Opposite leaf scars are shield shaped or half circular and generally do not surround the lateral bud.

Buds: Terminal bud is rounded, similar to white ash but slightly lighter colored with rusty brown pubescence on four imbricate bud scales. Lateral buds similar to terminals, but smaller.

Bark: Smooth and gray on young trees, becoming fissured with interlacing ridges—similar to some hickories or black walnut—with age. Also similar to white ash, but darker colored.

Fruits: Single-winged yellowish-brown samaras, generally less than 2 inches long, borne in drooping clusters. Very similar to white ash, except the samara wing wraps halfway around the seed.

Similar species in winter: White ash (page 30).

PRINCESSTREE

Scrophulariaceae
Paulownia tomentosa

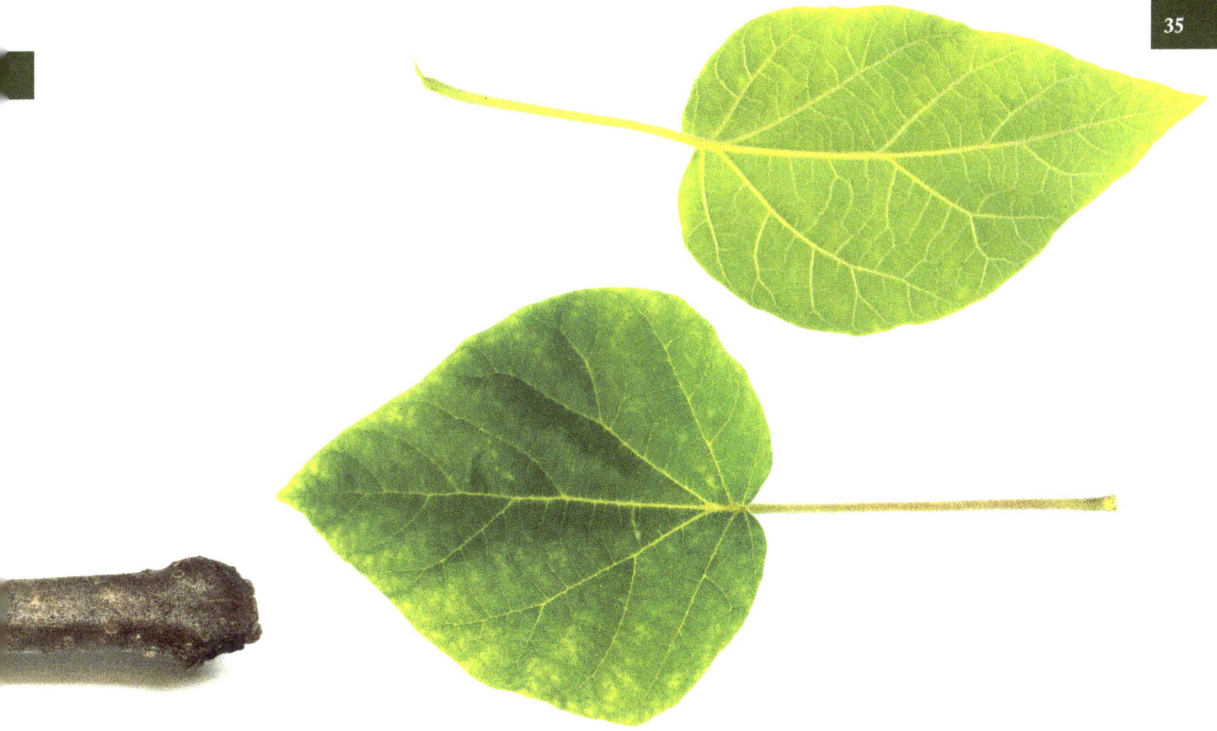

GENERAL DESCRIPTION

A small- to medium-sized tree, up to 50 feet tall. Often poorly formed, with a short trunk and several stout branches. Commonly found in disturbed sites and along roadsides and fencerows. Occasionally planted as an ornamental tree. Large, heart-shaped leaves are simple opposite and covered with a velvety pubescence.

WINTER ID FEATURES

Twig and leaf scars: Stout and brittle, light brown in color. Opposite leaf scars are circular, but less concave than southern catalpa. Abundant bundle scars visible. Hollow pith.

Buds: Terminal buds are absent. Lateral buds are small, round, and located above the circular leaf scars.

Bark: Grayish-brown and thin, developing shallow fissures with age.

Fruits: An ovoid capsule, similar in size and shape to a pecan, borne in large clusters, splitting to release thousands of tiny wind-dispersed seeds. Fruits persist through the winter and can be an excellent feature for identification.

Similar species in winter: Southern catalpa (page 22).

GENERAL KEY

GROUP 2

ALTERNATE LEAF SCARS

WHITE OAK

Fagaceae
Quercus alba

GENERAL DESCRIPTION

A large tree, up to 100 feet tall and several feet in diameter, with large, heavy branches and an often broad crown. Common in both the Piedmont and mountains, in a wide variety of sites—from dry to fairly moist—and usually found amongst other species of oaks, hickories, and other hardwoods. Simple alternate leaves are up to 9 inches long, with up to 10 rounded lobes. Lobing is very distinct on sun leaves.

WINTER ID FEATURES

Twig and leaf scars: Slender to moderately stout, grayish to grayish-red, glabrous and often lustrous, with small, half-circular leaf scars containing small bundle scars.

Buds: Terminal buds are small and rounded, clustered at the end of the twig, with glabrous reddish-brown imbricate bud scales. Lateral buds similar but usually smaller.

Bark: Light gray in color, somewhat scaly on smaller trees, developing large, flaky, exfoliating plates with age.

Fruits: An elongated acorn, up to 0.75 inch long, brown at maturity with a scaly cap that covers about a quarter of the nut. Like all members of the white oak group, acorns mature in the first growing season and can germinate shortly afterward—thus, newly germinated acorns can sometimes be found in winter below mature trees.

Similar species in winter: Overcup oak (page 46), bur oak (page 48), and post oak (page 62).

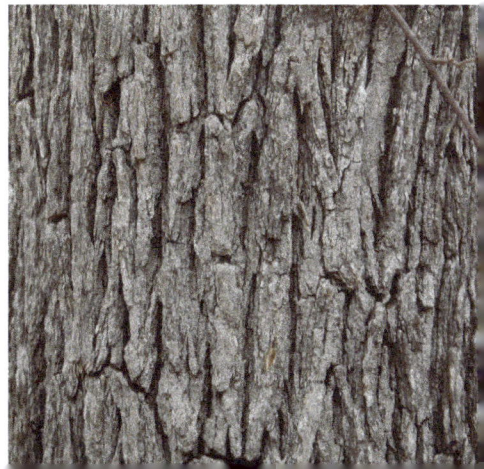

SCARLET OAK

Fagaceae
Quercus coccinea

GENERAL DESCRIPTION

A medium to large tree, up to 80 feet tall, usually with a poor form, irregular crown, and persistent dead branches. Common in both the Piedmont and mountains, particularly on drier upper slopes and ridges, mixed with other oaks, hickories, and yellow pines. Simple alternate leaves are up to 8 inches long, with distinctive C-shaped sinuses and seven to nine pointy, bristle-tipped lobes.

WINTER ID FEATURES

Twig and leaf scars: Moderately stout, reddish-brown, and glabrous, with small, half-circular leaf scars containing small bundle scars.

Buds: Terminal buds are fairly large (up to 0.25 inch long) and pointed, clustered at the end of the twig, with "frosty" pubescence at the tip. Imbricate scales clearly visible. Lateral buds similar but usually smaller.

Bark: Smooth and grayish-brown when young, developing rough, deep furrows and ridges with age. Light-colored, almost silvery, streaks sometimes visible on upper trunk.

Fruits: A spherical acorn, usually about 0.75 inch across, brown at maturity with a scaly cap that covers about half of the nut. The bottom of the acorn usually has a bullseye-like series of concentric rings. Like all members of the red oak group, acorns mature in the second growing season and require a winter chilling period before germinating. Ungerminated acorns sometimes found in winter below mature trees.

Similar species in winter: Water oak (page 54), black oak (page 64), northern red oak (page 60), blackjack oak (page 50), and pin oak (page 56).

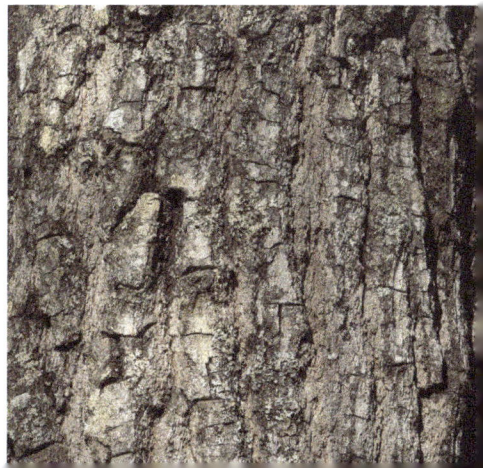

SOUTHERN RED OAK

Fagaceae
Quercus falcata

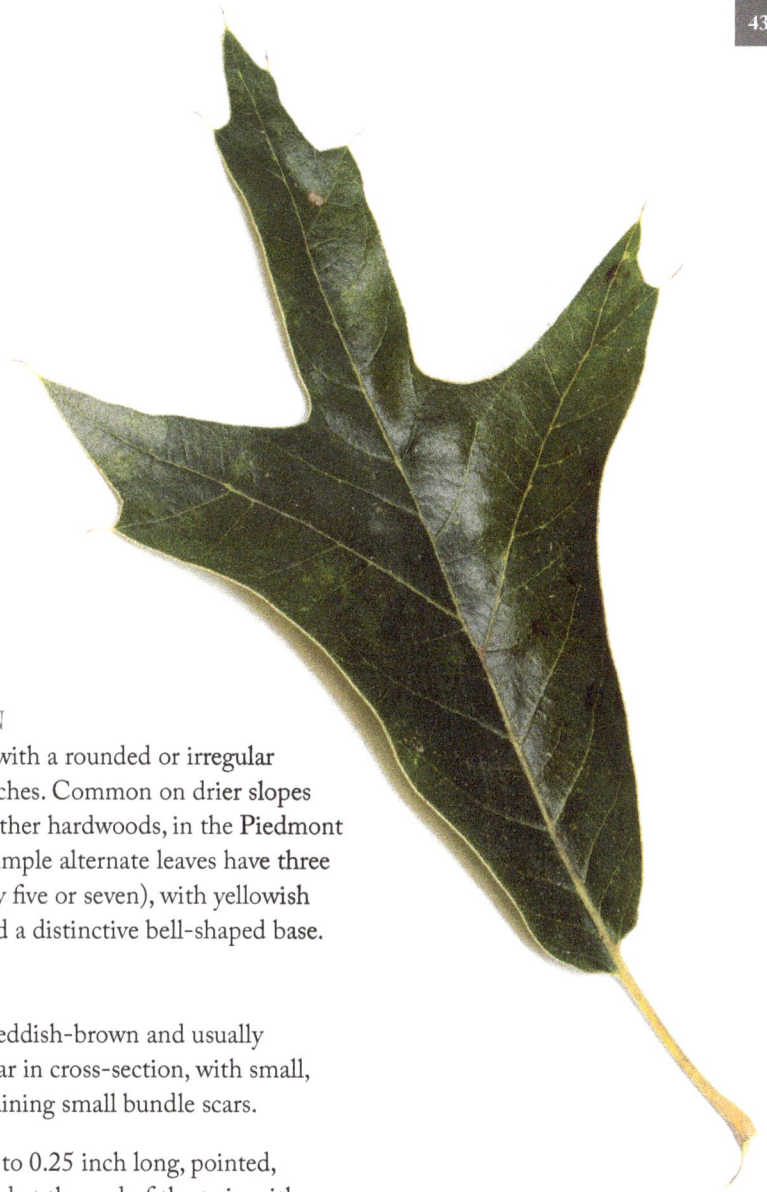

GENERAL DESCRIPTION

A large tree, up to 100 feet tall, with a rounded or irregular crown and large, spreading branches. Common on drier slopes and ridges, usually mixed with other hardwoods, in the Piedmont and low-elevation mountains. Simple alternate leaves have three to seven lobes (sun leaves usually five or seven), with yellowish pubescence on the underside and a distinctive bell-shaped base.

WINTER ID FEATURES

Twig and leaf scars: Stout, reddish-brown and usually pubescent, somewhat angular in cross-section, with small, half-circular leaf scars containing small bundle scars.

Buds: Terminal buds are up to 0.25 inch long, pointed, reddish-brown, and clustered at the end of the twig with pubescent imbricate scales. Lateral buds similar to terminals, but slightly smaller.

Bark: Dark grayish-brown to almost black, very thick, with rough, irregular ridges and deep furrows.

Fruits: A spherical, pubescent, reddish-brown acorn, up to 0.5 inch across, with a scaly cap covering about a third of the nut. Like all members of the red oak group, acorns mature in the second growing season and require a winter chilling period before germinating. Ungerminated acorns sometimes found in winter below mature trees.

Similar species in winter: Blackjack oak (page 50), black oak (page 64), northern red oak (page 60), shingle oak (page 44), and bur oak (page 48).

SHINGLE OAK

Fagaceae
Quercus imbricaria

GENERAL DESCRIPTION

A small- to medium-sized tree, up to 70 feet tall, with a straight trunk and rounded crown. Primarily a Midwestern species, but it occurs sporadically in the Piedmont and mountains, primarily in wetland fringes, stream banks, and bottomlands. Simple alternate leaves are elliptical or lanceolate in shape, up to 7 inches long, with a small bristle tip, and tardily deciduous.

WINTER ID FEATURES

Twig and leaf scars: Slender, reddish-brown, and glabrous (sometimes lustrous), with small, half-circular leaf scars containing small bundle scars.

Buds: Terminal buds are up to 0.25 inch long, rounded, grayish-yellow, and clustered at the end of the twig with pubescent imbricate scales. Lateral buds similar to terminals, but slightly smaller.

Bark: Smooth and gray when young, becoming dark grayish-brown, with shallow furrows developing with age. Purplish inner bark sometimes visible in the furrows of larger trees.

Fruits: A spherical, reddish-brown acorn, up to 0.75 inch across, with a scaly cap covering about a third of the nut. Faint striping sometimes visible on the acorn. Like all members of the red oak group, acorns mature in the second growing season and require a winter chilling period before germinating. Ungerminated acorns sometimes found in winter below mature trees.

Similar species in winter: Southern red oak (page 42), water oak (page 54), and willow oak (page 58).

OVERCUP OAK

Fagaceae
Quercus lyrata

GENERAL DESCRIPTION

A medium-sized tree, up to 80 feet tall, with an irregular crown unless grown in the open. Overcup oak is primarily a Coastal Plain species, but is occasionally found in floodplains and bottomlands in the Piedmont. Also commonly used as a landscaping and street tree, especially in the Piedmont but also in the mountains. Simple and alternate leaves are stiff, up to 10 inches long, with up to nine lobes and a roughly crucifix shape. Fine white pubescence found on the underside of the leaf.

WINTER ID FEATURES

Twig and leaf scars: Slender, grayish to grayish-red, glabrous and often lustrous, with small, half-circular leaf scars containing small bundle scars. Similar to white oak.

Buds: Terminal buds are small (0.125 inch long) and somewhat rounded, clustered at the end of the twig, with pubescent reddish-brown imbricate bud scales. Lateral buds similar, but usually smaller.

Bark: Similar to white oak, but thinner, and usually with abundant epicormic branches.

Fruits: A large spherical acorn, up to 1 inch across, completely (or nearly so) housed in a rough, scaly cap. Like all members of the white oak group, acorns mature in the first growing season and can germinate shortly afterward—thus, newly germinated acorns can sometimes be found in winter below mature trees.

Similar species in winter: White oak (page 38), bur oak (page 48), and post oak (page 62).

BUR OAK

Fagaceae
Quercus macrocarpa

GENERAL DESCRIPTION

A large tree, up to 90 feet tall and several feet in diameter, with a broad, spreading crown. Primarily found west of the Appalachians, but it occurs very sporadically in the Piedmont and mountains, usually planted. Simple alternate up to 10 inches long, with up to nine rounded lobes (terminal lobe usually largest), with a pubescent underside.

WINTER ID FEATURES

Twig and leaf scars: Very stout, grayish-brown in color, sometimes with tinges of yellow, with large, half-circular leaf scars containing small bundle scars. Small stipules sometimes present.

Buds: Terminal buds are up to 0.25 inch long, rounded, grayish-yellow, and clustered at the end of the twig with pubescent imbricate scales. Lateral buds similar to terminals, but slightly smaller.

Bark: Grayish-brown and scaly, similar to white oak, when young, becoming darker and deeply furrowed with age.

Fruits: A large, spherical acorn, up to 2 inches across, with a distinctive fringed cap covering up to three quarters of the nut. Like all members of the white oak group, acorns mature in the first growing season and can germinate shortly afterward—thus, newly germinated acorns can sometimes be found in winter below mature trees.

Similar species in winter: Southern red oak (page 42), white oak (page 38), overcup oak (page 46), and post oak (page 62).

BLACKJACK OAK

Fagaceae
Quercus marilandica

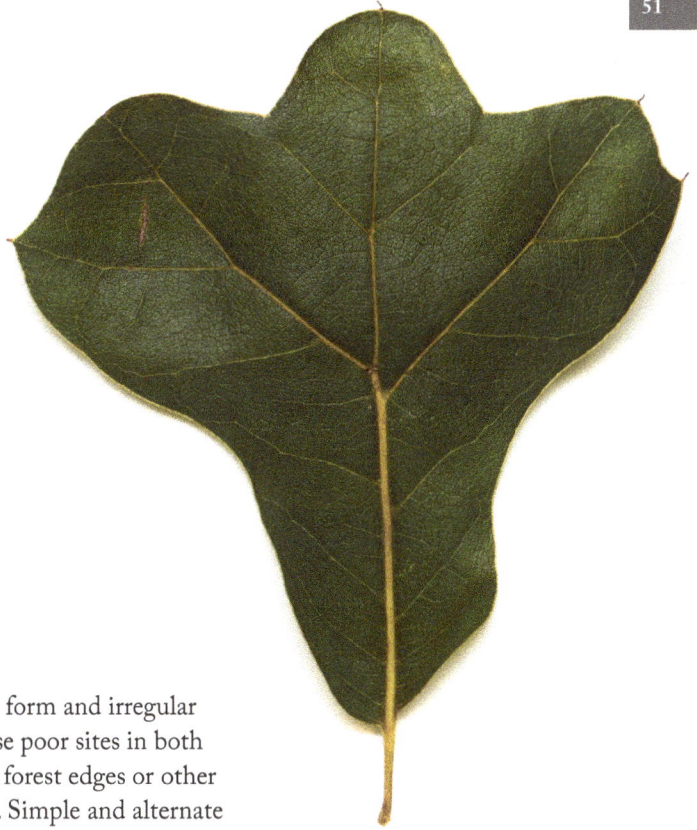

GENERAL DESCRIPTION

A small tree, up to 40 feet tall, with a poor form and irregular crown. Common on dry, rocky, or otherwise poor sites in both the Piedmont and mountains, typically on forest edges or other areas where it has access to direct sunlight. Simple and alternate leaves are up to 8 inches long, sometimes broadly spatulate, or with three rounded, bristle-tipped lobes. Leaf underside is covered with a coarse yellowish-brown pubescence.

WINTER ID FEATURES

Twig and leaf scars: Stout, grayish-brown, and slightly pubescent, with small, half-circular leaf scars containing small bundle scars.

Buds: Terminal buds are fairly large (up to 0.375 inch long), angular in cross-section, clustered at the end of the twig, with imbricate scales densely covered with tan or rusty pubescence. Lateral buds similar to terminals, and diverging from the twig at a 45-degree angle.

Bark: Thick, rough, and nearly black, often developing blocky plates with age.

Fruits: A slightly oblong acorn, up to 0.75 inch long, covered with fine pubescence. Scaly cap covers about half of the nut. Like all members of the red oak group, acorns mature in the second growing season and require a winter chilling period before germinating. Ungerminated acorns sometimes found in winter below mature trees.

Similar species in winter: Black oak (page 64), scarlet oak (page 40), and southern red oak (page 42).

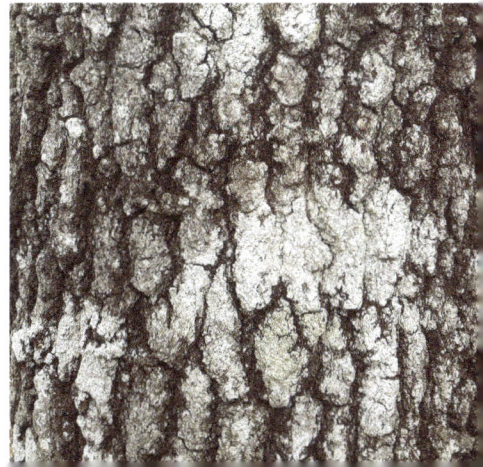

CHESTNUT OAK

Fagaceae
Quercus montana

GENERAL DESCRIPTION

A medium- to large-sized tree, up to 80 feet tall, often with a crooked stem and narrow or irregular crown. Common on drier upper slopes and ridges, often mixed with yellow pines, primarily in the mountains, but occasionally in the Piedmont. Simple and alternate leaves are elliptical in shape, up to 8 inches long, with a crenate margin.

WINTER ID FEATURES

Twig and leaf scars: Moderately stout, reddish-brown, and glabrous, with small, half-circular leaf scars containing small bundle scars.

Buds: Terminal buds are long (up to 0.5 inch), thin, and pointed, clustered at the end of the twig, with imbricate scales covered with tan pubescence. Lateral buds similar to terminals, and diverging from the twig at a 45-degree angle.

Bark: Smooth and grayish-brown when young, becoming much thicker with deep furrows with age.

Fruits: A large, slightly oblong acorn, yellow when fresh, becoming reddish-brown after dropping, up to 1.5 inches long, with a scaly cap covering about half of the nut. Like all members of the white oak group, acorns mature in the first growing season and can germinate shortly afterward—thus, newly germinated acorns can sometimes be found in winter below mature trees.

Similar species in winter: Black oak (page 64).

WATER OAK

Fagaceae
Quercus nigra

GENERAL DESCRIPTION

A medium-sized tree, occasionally up to 100 feet tall, with a broad, spreading crown. Common on a range of sites, from floodplains and bottomlands to drier uplands, in the Piedmont and low-elevation mountains. Simple alternate leaves are spatulate in shape, up to 4 inches long, and tardily deciduous.

WINTER ID FEATURES

Twig and leaf scars: Slender and reddish-brown, with small, half-circular leaf scars containing small bundle scars.

Buds: Terminal buds are short, up to 0.25 inch long, thin, and pointed, clustered at the end of the twig, with "frosty" pubescence at the tip, similar to scarlet oak. Imbricate scales clearly visible. Lateral buds similar to terminals, and diverging from the twig at a 45-degree angle.

Bark: Smooth and gray when young, becoming darker with slight furrows developing with age. Orangeish-red inner bark sometimes visible in the furrows of larger trees.

Fruits: A spherical acorn, up to 0.5 inch across, with a scaly cap covering about half of the nut. Like all members of the "red oak" group, acorns mature in the second growing season and require a winter chilling period before germinating. Ungerminated acorns sometimes found in winter below mature trees.

Similar species in winter: Willow oak (page 58), shingle oak (page 44), and scarlet oak (page 40).

PIN OAK
Fagaceae
Quercus palustris

GENERAL DESCRIPTION

A medium-sized tree, up to 80 feet tall, with a straight trunk and a rounded, open canopy. Sporadically found in the Piedmont and mountains, particularly on wet sites. Also commonly planted as a landscaping or street tree across the region. Simple and alternate leaves are up to 5 inches long, have up to seven bristle-tipped lobes, and deep, rounded sinuses.

WINTER ID FEATURES

Twig and leaf scars: Slender and reddish-brown, with small, half-circular leaf scars containing small bundle scars.

Buds: Terminal buds are very small (up to 0.125 inch long), thin, and pointed, clustered at the end of the twig, with glabrous reddish-brown imbricate scales. Lateral buds similar to terminals, but smaller.

Bark: Grayish-brown and thin, developing shallow ridges and furrows with age. Short, peg-like dead branches often found on the trunk.

Fruits: A spherical acorn, up to 0.5 inch across, with a scaly cap covering about a quarter of the nut. Slight pubescence and faint stripes sometimes visible on the nut. Like all members of the red oak group, acorns mature in the second growing season and require a winter chilling period before germinating. Ungerminated acorns sometimes found in winter below mature trees.

Similar species in winter: Scarlet oak (page 40) northern red oak (page 60), and willow oak (page 58).

WILLOW OAK

Fagaceae
Quercus phellos

GENERAL DESCRIPTION

A large, fast-growing tree, up to 100 feet tall, with a rounded crown and a straight trunk. Common in wet sites in the Piedmont, like floodplains and bottomlands, and also regularly used as a landscaping or street tree. Infrequent in the mountains. Simple alternate leaves are narrowly elliptical or lanceolate in shape, up to 5 inches long, with a small bristle tip, and tardily deciduous.

WINTER ID FEATURES

Twig and leaf scars: Very slender, brown to grayish-brown, and generally hairless, with small, half-circular leaf scars containing small bundle scars.

Buds: Terminal buds are up to 0.125 inch long, pointed, and clustered at the end of the twig with glabrous brown imbricate scales. A small amount of pubescence sometimes visible at the tip. Lateral buds similar to terminals, but slightly smaller and diverging from the twig at a 45-degree angle.

Bark: Smooth and grayish-brown when young, becoming darker with slight furrows developing with age. Similar to water oak, but lacking the orangeish-brown inner bark in the furrows.

Fruits: A spherical acorn, up to 0.5 inch across, with a scaly cap covering just the very top of the nut (like a tiny northern red oak acorn). Like all members of the red oak group, acorns mature in the second growing season and require a winter chilling period before germinating. Ungerminated acorns sometimes found in winter below mature trees.

Similar species in winter: Water oak (page 54), shingle oak (page 44), and pin oak (page 56).

NORTHERN RED OAK

Fagaceae
Quercus rubra

GENERAL DESCRIPTION

A large tree, up to 100 feet tall, with a rounded crown and a
straight trunk. Sometimes develops a gnarled appearance, with a
shorter trunk, on exposed sites. Common in both the Piedmont
and mountains, typically mixed with other hardwoods—
although largely restricted to cool, moist, north facing slopes in
the Piedmont. Simple and alternate leaves are up to 8 inches
long, with five to seven bristle-tipped lobes. Leaves are similar to
scarlet oak, but the sinuses are not as distinctly C shaped.

WINTER ID FEATURES

Twig and leaf scars: Stout, reddish-brown, and glabrous,
sometimes with a lustrous bronzed appearance, with small,
half-circular leaf scars containing small bundle scars.

Buds: Terminal buds are up to 0.25 inch long, round in
cross-section, pointed, and clustered at the end of the twig
with glabrous reddish-brown imbricate scales. A small
amount of pubescence sometimes visible at the tip. Lateral
buds similar to terminals, but slightly smaller.

Bark: Gray or grayish-brown and smooth when young,
becoming deeply furrowed and darker gray, with light-
colored vertical stripes, with age.

Fruits: A spherical acorn, up to 1 inch across, with a scaly
cap covering just the very top of the nut (cap looks like a
tiny beret). Like all members of the red oak group, acorns
mature in the second growing season and require a winter
chilling period before germinating. Ungerminated acorns
sometimes found in winter below mature trees.

Similar species in winter: Scarlet oak (page 40), pin oak
(page 56), southern red oak (page 42).

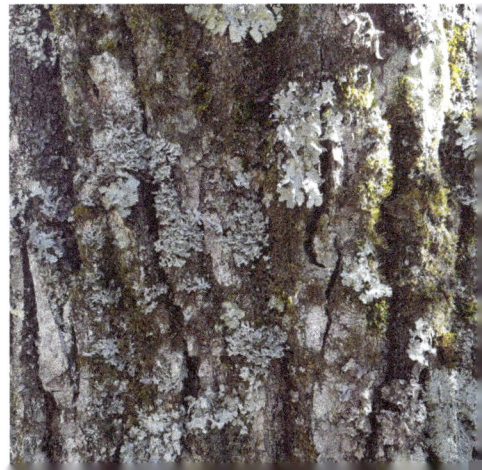

POST OAK
Fagaceae
Quercus stellata

GENERAL DESCRIPTION

A medium-sized tree, up to 70 feet tall, with large, crooked branches and an irregular crown. Common on drier upper slopes and ridges, usually mixed with other oaks and hickories, in the Piedmont and mountains. Simple and alternate leaves are up to 7 inches across with three to five lobes, often with a distinctive crucifix shape. Dense stellate (branched) pubescence is readily visible on the leaf underside.

WINTER ID FEATURES

Twig and leaf scars: Very stout and yellowish-gray, usually with some pubescence near the tip. Leaf scars are fairly large, half circular, and contain many bundle scars.

Buds: Terminal buds are short (up to 0.125 inch long) and rounded, clustered at the end of the twig with pubescent orangeish-brown imbricate bud scales. Lateral buds similar to terminals, but smaller.

Bark: Light gray in color, somewhat scaly on smaller trees, developing large, flaky, exfoliating plates with age. Similar to white oak.

Fruits: A spherical acorn, up to 0.75 inch across, with a scaly cap covering about half of the nut. Like all members of the white oak group, acorns mature in the first growing season and can germinate shortly afterward—thus, newly germinated acorns can sometimes be found in winter below mature trees.

Similar species in winter: Overcup oak (page 46), bur oak (page 48), and white oak (page 38).

BLACK OAK
Fagaceae
Quercus velutina

GENERAL DESCRIPTION

A large tree, up to 90 feet tall, with a broad, irregular crown and large, heavy branches. Common in both the Piedmont and mountains, particularly on drier upper slopes and ridges, mixed with other oaks, hickories, and yellow pines. Simple and alternate leaves are up to 8 inches long, with five to seven bristle-tipped lobes. Lobing is often much less distinct on shade leaves and on smaller individuals.

WINTER ID FEATURES

Twig and leaf scars: Stout, reddish-brown, and lustrous, usually hairless, somewhat angular in cross-section, with small, half-circular leaf scars containing small bundle scars.

Buds: Terminal buds are large, up to 0.5 inch long, angular, pointed, and clustered at the end of the twig with imbricate scales covered in dense tan pubescence. Lateral buds similar to terminals, but slightly smaller.

Bark: Smooth and gray or grayish-brown when young, becoming deeply furrowed and dark gray (almost black) with age. Yellowish-orange inner bark sometimes visible in the furrows.

Fruits: A spherical acorn, up to 0.75 inches across, with a scaly cap covering more than half of the nut. Like all members of the red oak group, acorns mature in the second growing season and require a winter chilling period before germinating. Ungerminated acorns sometimes found in winter below mature trees.

Similar species in winter: Blackjack oak (page 50), southern red oak (page 42), scarlet oak (page 40), and chestnut oak (page 52).

YELLOW BIRCH

Betulaceae
Betula alleghaniensis

GENERAL DESCRIPTION

Occasionally a large tree, approaching 100 feet, but usually smaller. A major component of northern hardwood forests in the northeastern United States; restricted to mid- to high-elevation mountains in the southern Appalachians. Alternate, ovate leaves are faintly doubly serrate, with an inequilateral (asymmetrical), rounded, or heart-shaped base. Leaves can be clustered on the end of the twig, appearing whorled, or widely spaced on long shoots.

WINTER ID FEATURES

Twig and leaf scars: Slender, zigzag twigs, greenish-brown in color, with horizontal lenticels. Short spur shoots often present on older trees. Distinctive wintergreen smell when crushed.

Buds: Sharply pointed reddish-brown buds with imbricate scales. Fine ciliate hairs typically present.

Bark: Golden or bronze colored and smooth on young trees, peeling in thin, papery, horizontal strips. Rough, scaly, and reddish-brown or gray on larger trees.

Fruits: Male flowers are small, drooping catkins, generally less than 2 inches long. Female fruits, found on the same tree, are cone like, upright, and present in late fall and early winter.

Similar species in winter: Black birch (page 68), eastern hophornbeam (page 158), and river birch (page 70).

BLACK BIRCH

Betulaceae
Betula lenta

GENERAL DESCRIPTION

A medium-sized to large tree, approaching 80 feet, but usually smaller. A component of northern hardwood forests in the northeastern United States; restricted to mid- to high-elevation mountains in the southern Appalachians. Alternate, ovate leaves are faintly singly or faintly doubly serrate, with an inequilateral (asymmetrical), rounded, or heart-shaped base. Leaves can be clustered on the end of the twig, appearing whorled, or widely spaced on long shoots.

WINTER ID FEATURES

Twig and leaf scars: Slender, zigzag twigs, reddish-brown in color, with horizontal lenticels. Short spur shoots often present on older trees. Distinctive wintergreen smell when crushed.

Buds: Sharply pointed reddish-brown or green and brown buds with imbricate scales. Similar to yellow birch, but lacking ciliate hairs.

Bark: Reddish-brown and smooth on young trees, somewhat resembling a young black cherry. Does not peel and flake like yellow birch. Becomes gray to black with age, and develops large, flattened scaly plates.

Fruits: Male flowers are small, drooping catkins, generally less than 2 inches long. Female fruits, found on the same tree, are cone like, upright, and present in late fall and early winter. Similar to yellow birch.

Similar species in winter: Yellow birch (page 66), eastern hophornbeam (page 158), and river birch (page 70).

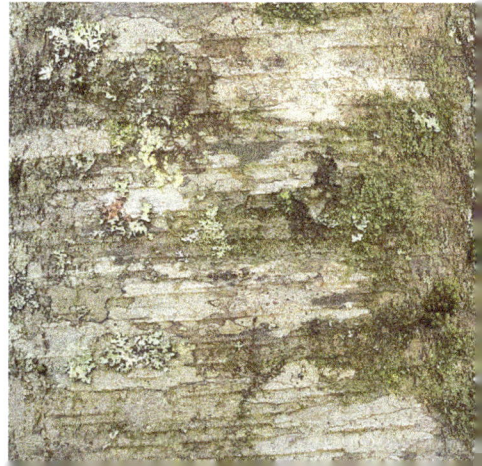

RIVER BIRCH
Betulaceae
Betula nigra

GENERAL DESCRIPTION

A medium-sized tree, occasionally up to 80 feet tall, often with multiple trunks and drooping branches. Native to lower slopes and floodplains, and is more common in the Piedmont than in the mountains. Also frequently used as a landscape tree. Simple and alternate leaves are ovate in shape, with an abruptly truncate base and doubly serrated margin.

WINTER ID FEATURES

Twig and leaf scars: Slender and zigzag, brown or reddish-brown in color, sometimes with short spur shoots, and usually with abundant raised white lenticels that feel like sandpaper. Occasionally has a fine pubescence. Leaf scars are crescent shaped and contain three small bundle scars. Twigs lack the wintergreen smell characteristic of black birch and yellow birch.

Buds: Terminal buds are absent; lateral buds are pointed, up to 0.25 inch long, with three slightly pubescent imbricate bud scales.

Bark: Smooth when young, often with a slight reddish- or golden hue, becoming grayer and developing thick exfoliating plates with age.

Fruits: Small (up to 1.5 inches long) cone-like aggregates of tiny nuts. Fruits mature in the fall and typically do not persist into winter.

Similar species in winter: Black birch (page 68) and yellow birch (page 66).

BLACKGUM

Cornaceae
Nyssa sylvatica

GENERAL DESCRIPTION

A large tree, up to 100 feet in height, with a dense irregular crown and distinctive horizontal branching pattern. Widely distributed across a range of Piedmont and mountain sites, and often locally abundant, mixed with oaks, hickories, and other hardwoods. Simple alternate leaves are oblong to elliptical in shape, up to 5 inches long, occasionally having one or two shallow lobes.

WINTER ID FEATURES

Twig and leaf scars: Fairly stout, glabrous, gray to grayish-brown in color, with prominent light-colored lenticels. Leaf scars half circular, with three distinctive bundle scars within, giving it a "sloth face" appearance.

Buds: Terminal buds up to 0.25 inch long, with reddish-brown (sometimes purplish), glabrous imbricate bud scales. Lateral buds smaller and often absent.

Bark: Ranging from gray to dark grayish-brown, scaly or irregularly furrowed when young, sometimes developing a blocky "alligator skin"-like appearance (similar to common persimmon) when large.

Fruits: A dark purplish to black drupe, sometimes with a glaucous appearance, borne in small hanging clusters. Fruits mature in early fall and rarely persist into the winter.

Similar species in winter: Common persimmon (page 160), sourwood (page 162), and sweetgum (page 120).

AMERICAN BEECH
Fagaceae
Fagus grandifolia

GENERAL DESCRIPTION

A sometimes massive tree, often 100 feet tall and more than 3 feet in diameter. Common on moist sites in the Piedmont and low- to mid-elevation mountains. Also occurs on drier sites, but typically does not grow large there. Simple, elliptical leaves are 3–5 inches long, with straight, parallel veins terminating in pointed teeth at the margin.

WINTER ID FEATURES

Twig and leaf scars: Slender and zigzag in appearance, light brown or sometimes grayish in color. Senescent leaves often persistent until mid-winter. Small shield-shaped or half-circular leaf scars.

Buds: Long (up to 1 inch), pointy buds, tan or light reddish-brown, with numerous distinctive imbricate scales. Buds diverge from the twig at a broad angle.

Bark: Gray and smooth, even on large stems. Sometimes splotchy, and often disfigured by vandals and disease.

Fruits: Paired, wedge-shaped or triangular nuts, housed in a small (less than 1 inch) tan-colored spiny bur. Sometimes abundant in fall and winter.

Similar species in winter: Downy serviceberry (page 78) and yellowwood (page 98).

RED MULBERRY

Moraceae
Morus rubra

GENERAL DESCRIPTION

A small tree, occasionally reaching 60 feet in height, with a short trunk and broad, spreading branches. Widely distributed across a range of Piedmont and mountain sites, but typically not abundant. Large leaves, up to 5 inches across, have serrated margins and a distinctive scabrous texture. Leaves are trimorphic; most are ovate or heart shaped, but some might have two lobes, others three.

WINTER ID FEATURES

Twig and leaf scars: Slender and zigzag, yellowish-brown to reddish-brown in color, exuding a milky sap when cut. Leaf scars are small, sunken and half circle shaped.

Buds: Pointed buds up to 0.25 inch across, with six to seven imbricate bud scales. Buds very similar to American basswood, but the latter only has two to three scales and lacks the pointy tip.

Bark: Gray to reddish-brown, smooth when young, developing thin scaly plates with age.

Fruits: A fleshy cluster of drupes, up to 2 inches long, similar to a large blackberry. Fruits mature in summer and are typically not present in winter

Similar species in winter: Basswood (page 86) and Osage-orange (page 116).

DOWNY SERVICEBERRY

Rosaceae
Amelanchier arborea

GENERAL DESCRIPTION

A shrub or small tree (rarely more than 40 feet tall), typically
with a narrow, irregularly shaped crown. An occasional midstory
tree across a range of Piedmont sites. Rarer in the mountains.
Elliptical leaves with a pointed tip, similar to black cherry but
with a rounded or heart-shaped base. Attractive white flowers
emerge before the leaves and can aid with winter identification.

WINTER ID FEATURES

Twig and leaf scars: Slender brownish or gray-brown twigs,
occasionally with pubescence. Crescent or slightly V-shaped
leaf scars, with three visible bundle scars within.

Buds: Elongated and pointed terminal buds (more than 0.5
inch) and slightly smaller appressed laterals. Imbricate scales,
often with fine pubescence on margins and tips. Color
ranges from pinkish-green in late fall to reddish-brown in
late winter.

Bark: Smooth and gray, becoming slightly furrowed with
age.

Fruits: Small reddish or purple pomes, maturing in early
summer, generally not present in winter.

Similar species in winter: American beech (page 74) and
black cherry (page 178).

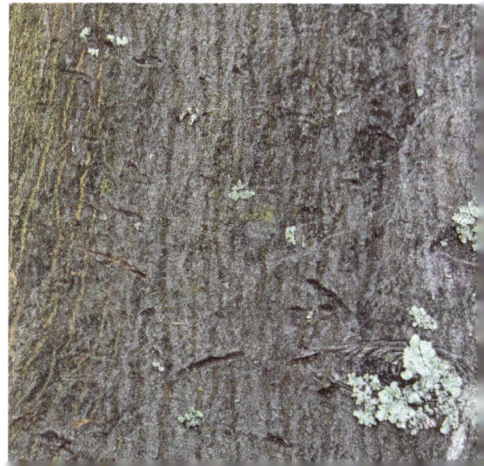

CALLERY PEAR

Rosaceae
Pyrus calleryana

GENERAL DESCRIPTION

A small- to medium-sized tree, usually with a short trunk, upright branches, and a rounded or conical crown. Native to Asia, but widely planted across the region as a landscape plant, and increasingly recognized as invasive. Simple alternate leaves are ovate or slightly heart shaped, up to 3 inches across, with a finely serrated margin.

WINTER ID FEATURES

Twig and leaf scars: Fairly stout and reddish-brown, with hints of gray. Large, thorny spur shoots up to 4 inches long (usually shorter) are sometimes present. Small, half-circular leaf scars.

Buds: Terminal buds are large, up to 0.5 inch long, with imbricate scales densely covered with silky tan-colored hairs.

Bark: Smooth, gray, and cherry like, with prominent lenticels when young, becoming light brown to grayish-brown with scaly ridges with age.

Fruits: A small apple-like pome, about 0.5 inch in diameter, brown in color, hanging from a short stalk.

Similar species in winter: Hawthorn (page 118).

EASTERN COTTONWOOD
Salicaceae
Populus deltoides

GENERAL DESCRIPTION

A large tree, up to 100 feet tall and several feet in diameter, usually with a long, straight trunk and an open, spreading crown. Found primarily in floodplains and bottomlands, especially in the Piedmont. Infrequent in the mountains. Simple alternate leaves are triangular, with a coarsely toothed or scalloped margin and a distinctive flattened petiole.

WINTER ID FEATURES

Twig and leaf scars: Stout, somewhat triangular in cross-section, and yellowish-green or gray in color. Leaf scar somewhat three lobed, with visible bundle scars. Stipular scars usually visible.

Buds: Buds are large (up to 0.75 inch long), covered with lustrous green or greenish-brown imbricate scales that can be somewhat sticky.

Bark: Smooth and gray when young, becoming deeply furrowed—similar to that of a large yellow poplar—with age.

Fruits: A small brown capsule that opens to release tiny, cottony, wind-dispersed seeds. Matures in summer and typically not present in winter.

Similar species in winter: Sweetgum (page 120) and yellow-poplar (page 108).

HORSESUGAR

Symplocaceae
Symplocos tinctoria

GENERAL DESCRIPTION

A shrub or small tree, occasionally 25 feet tall, typically with a short trunk and ascending branches. Primarily found in moist sites in the Piedmont and Coastal Plain, although it is locally abundant along the Blue Ridge Escarpment. Simple and alternate leaves are tardily deciduous, elliptical in shape, with faint teeth on the margin and a yellow midvein. Leaves have a sweet taste.

WINTER ID FEATURES

Twig and leaf scars: Fairly stout and reddish-brown in color, covered in fine pubescence. Leaf scars are crescent shaped and contain a single large bundle scar.

Buds: Terminal buds are large and pointed, with three to four pubescent imbricate bud scales. Lateral buds are much smaller and often not visible. Preformed flower buds, often visible in the winter, are spherical, about 0.25 inch across, with a fringe of ciliate hairs on the margins.

Bark: Gray to grayish-brown with scattered lenticels when young, becoming darker and developing shallow furrows with age.

Fruits: Small, elongated brown drupes, up to 0.5 inch long. Fruits mature in late summer and rarely persist into winter.

Similar species in winter: Sweetbay magnolia (page 174).

BASSWOOD

Tiliaceae
Tilia americana

GENERAL DESCRIPTION

A large tree, up to 100 feet tall, often with a straight trunk, broad crown, arching branches, and abundant basal sprouts. Commonly found across the Piedmont and mountains, particularly in fertile, moist sites. Simple alternate leaves are roughly heart shaped, up to 6 inches across, with a finely serrated margin and an asymmetrical base. There are three native varieties in the region (American basswood [*Tilia americana*], white basswood [*Tilia americana* var. *heterophylla*], and Carolina basswood [*Tilia americana* var. *caroliniana*]), distinguished primarily by leaf characteristics (var. *heterophylla* pictured). Varieties are largely indistinguishable in winter.

WINTER ID FEATURES

Twig and leaf scars: Fairly stout, zigzag, and reddish in color, often with hints of green in late fall and early winter. Leaf scars are half circular to slightly crescent shaped.

Buds: Terminal bud is absent; lateral buds are asymmetrical and rounded with two to three (occasionally four) imbricate bud scales.

Bark: Smooth and gray or grayish-green when young, becoming grayish-brown with flat ridges and shallow furrows with age.

Fruits: A small round nut, up to 0.25 inch in diameter, in stalked clusters below a narrow leaf-like bract. Fruits mature in the fall and often persist into winter.

Similar species in winter: Red mulberry (page 76).

AMERICAN SYCAMORE

Platanaceae
Plantanus occidentalis

GENERAL DESCRIPTION

A large tree up, to 100 feet tall and several feet in diameter, with an open, spreading crown. Widely distributed across the Piedmont and mountains, particularly in floodplains and alongside waterways. Also frequently planted as a landscaping or street tree. Simple alternate leaves with maple-like shape, up to 8 inches across, with three to five lobes.

WINTER ID FEATURES

Twig and leaf scars: Fairly stout, zigzag, greenish-gray in color (predominantly gray in winter), with stipular scars surrounding the twig. Leaf scar surrounds the bud and contains numerous round bundle scars.

Buds: Buds are large, reddish-brown, and pointy, covered with a single cap-like scale.

Bark: Mottled in appearance, often with patches of exfoliating gray or grayish-brown scales surrounded by areas of light gray (sometimes white) exposed inner bark. On larger trees, the upper trunks and branches are often predominantly white.

Fruits: Bumpy, spherical fruits, 0.75–1 inch across, hanging individually from 3- to 5-inch stalks. When broken or stepped on, they disintegrate into their component achenes—each with a bundle of stiff hairs attached. Fruits sometimes persist on the tree into the winter, or can be found on the ground.

Similar species in winter: None.

BLACK WILLOW

Salicaceae
Salix nigra

GENERAL DESCRIPTION

A shrub or tree, occasionally up to 100 feet tall and 2 feet
or more in diameter, with a spreading crown and slightly
downward-arching branches. Widespread across the Piedmont
and mountains, particularly in moist sites along floodplains,
wetland fringes, and stream banks. Simple alternate leaves are
lanceolate in shape, up to 7 inches long, with finely serrated
margins and a glaucous underside.

WINTER ID FEATURES

Twig and leaf scars: Slender, glabrous, and yellowish-brown
in color. Twigs snap off easily from the main branch. Small
leaf scars contain three faintly visible bundle scars.

Buds: Terminal buds absent; lateral buds small, covered with
a single cap-like bud scale, slightly beaked and appressed to
the twig.

Bark: Brownish-gray to almost black, fissuring into scaly
exfoliating plates on larger trees.

Fruits: A small capsule, approximately 0.25 inch across,
maturing in early to mid-summer and rarely persisting into
winter.

Similar species in winter: Silky willow (page 92).

SILKY WILLOW
Salicaceae
Salix sericea

GENERAL DESCRIPTION

A shrub or small tree, often multistemmed, rarely taller than 10 feet. Primarily a northeastern species, but sporadically found the Piedmont (north of South Carolina) and in the mountains, typically in moist sites. Simple alternate leaves are lanceolate in shape, up to 5 inches long, with finely serrated margins and silky pubescence on the underside.

WINTER ID FEATURES

Twig and leaf scars: Slender, zigzag, reddish-brown, and slightly glaucous, with scattered lenticels. Leaf scars thin and U shaped, containing small bundle scars.

Buds: Terminal buds absent; lateral buds small, covered with a single cap-like bud scale, slightly beaked and appressed to the twig.

Bark: Gray and smooth when young, with corky lenticels often present. Shallow fissures developing with age.

Fruits: A small capsule, approximately 0.25 inch across and covered with silky pubescence, maturing in summer and rarely persisting into winter.

Similar species in winter: Black willow (page 90).

PAWPAW

Annonaceae
Asimina triloba

GENERAL DESCRIPTION

A small tree, sometimes up to 30 feet tall but generally shorter, often forming clumps or dense thickets. A common understory tree in Piedmont mesic sites. Less frequent in the mountains. Alternate, obovate leaves are up to 12 inches long and have a distinctive green pepper smell when crushed.

WINTER ID FEATURES

Twig and leaf scars: Slender, light brown to reddish-brown, with rusty pubescence, often with a zigzag appearance. Crescent shaped leaf scars with five visible bundle scars. Twigs have a similar odor to leaves when crushed or scratched.

Buds: Terminal buds are naked, up to 0.5 inch long, and covered with rusty-red or maroon pubescence. Lateral buds smaller, rounder, and partially surrounded by leaf scar.

Bark: Dark brown, sometimes splotchy, with prominent lenticels.

Fruits: Large oblong or pear-shaped berries, up to 5 inches long, changing from green to brown as they approach maturity in the fall. Rarely present in winter.

Similar species in winter: Carolina buckthorn (page 104).

MOUNTAIN PEPPERBUSH

Clethraceae
Clethra acuminata

GENERAL DESCRIPTION

A multistemmed shrub or small tree, occasionally to 20 feet tall, with a sparse, irregular crown. Typically found at elevations between 2,500 and 4,000 feet on moist lower slopes, along streambanks, or in coves. Not found in the Piedmont. Simple and alternate leaves are elliptical in shape, with a finely serrated margin and a long, pointed tip.

WINTER ID FEATURES

Twig and leaf scars: Slender, grayish-brown and very pubescent, with a distinct triangular or crescent-shaped leaf scar containing a single large bundle scar.

Buds: Terminal buds are up to 0.25 inch long, and covered with silvery pubescent imbricate bud scales that extend beyond the tip of the bud, giving it a naked appearance. Lateral buds are much smaller, and partially submerged into the leaf scar.

Bark: Reddish-brown or cinnamon colored and smooth when young, exfoliating in papery strips on larger stems.

Fruits: Small, brown, peppercorn-like capsules, up to 0.125 inch across, borne in clusters on the flowering stalks. Similar to sourwood fruits but smaller. Fruits mature in the fall and persist through the winter.

Similar species in winter: None.

YELLOWWOOD

Fabaceae
Cladrastis kentukea

GENERAL DESCRIPTION

A medium-sized tree, up to 50 feet all, typically with a short trunk and a broad, spreading crown. Typically found in moist sites along streams, coves, or on lower slopes—particularly on calcareous soils in the southern Appalachians and westward. Odd-pinnately compound leaves, typically with seven or nine leaflets. Petiole base is swollen and covers the bud.

WINTER ID FEATURES

Twig and leaf scars: Slender and zigzag, glabrous, and slightly lustrous, brown or reddish-brown in color. Typically covered with small whitish lenticels. Leaf scars surround or nearly surround the buds and contain several large bundle scars.

Buds: Buds are cone shaped and naked, covered with a brownish pubescence.

Bark: Gray or slightly grayish-brown and smooth. Very similar to American beech.

Fruits: A thin, papery legume pod, up to 4 inches long, similar to the eastern redbud, sometimes persisting through the winter.

Similar species in winter: American beech (page 74) and eastern redbud (page 166).

WITCHHAZEL
Hamamelidaceae
Hamamelis virginiana

GENERAL DESCRIPTION

A shrub or small tree, up to 30–35 feet tall, typically with a short trunk and irregular crown. Most commonly found in moist sites, particularly along the edge of streams or wetlands, in both the Piedmont and mountains. Simple and alternate leaves are variable in shape (mostly obovate), with scalloped and slightly wavy margins and scattered hairs on the underside.

WINTER ID FEATURES

Twig and leaf scars: Slender, zigzag, and reddish-brown in color, often covered in small loose scales. Small three-lobed leaf scars with three bundle scars within.

Buds: A naked stalked bud up to 0.5 inch long, covered in fine brown hairs. Small circular flower buds are often present in late fall, before flowering in the winter.

Bark: Light brown to gray, smooth when young and becoming slightly scaly with age. In wetter environments, bark texture is often obscured by mosses and algae.

Fruits: An irregularly shaped woody capsule, up to 0.5 inch across, exploding forcefully in the fall to disperse two small black seeds. Empty capsules may persist on the tree through the winter.

Similar species in winter: Hazel alder (page 106).

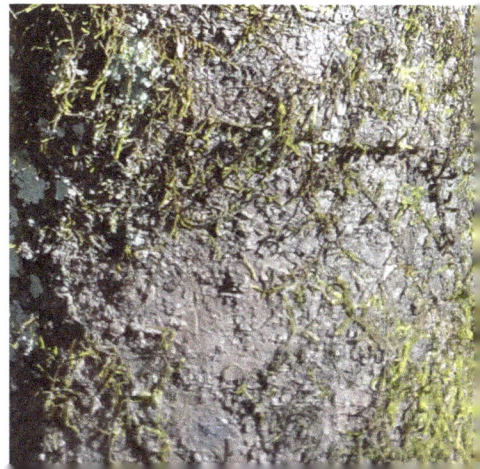

BITTERNUT HICKORY

Juglandaceae
Carya cordiformis

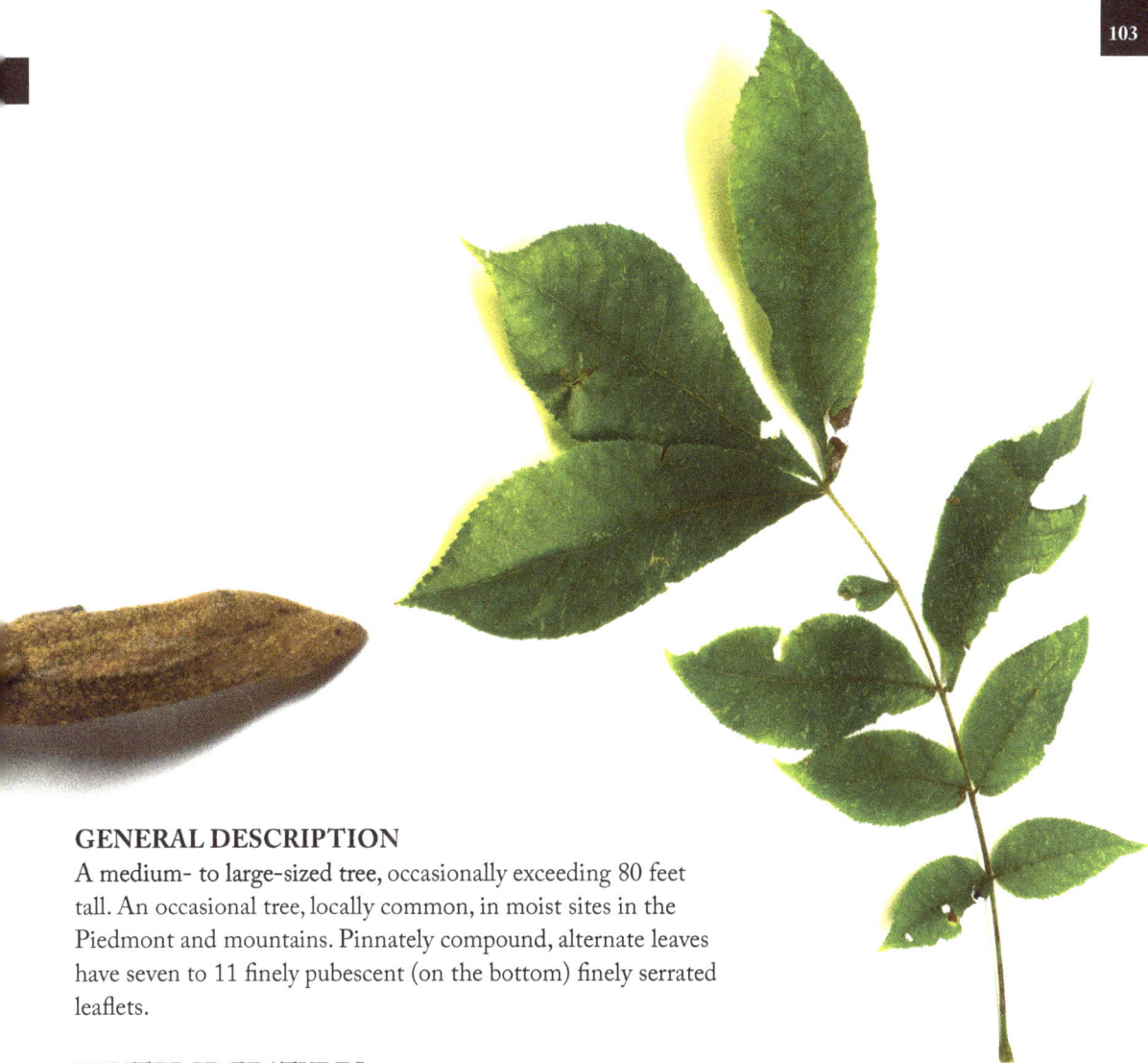

GENERAL DESCRIPTION

A medium- to large-sized tree, occasionally exceeding 80 feet tall. An occasional tree, locally common, in moist sites in the Piedmont and mountains. Pinnately compound, alternate leaves have seven to 11 finely pubescent (on the bottom) finely serrated leaflets.

WINTER ID FEATURES

Twig and leaf scars: Slender, relative to other hickories, orange-brown or yellowish in appearance, with three-lobed leaf scars.

Buds: Terminal buds are flattened, up to 0.5 inch long, covered with a sulphur-yellow/brown pubescence, and appear naked (they are actually valvate). Lateral buds similar, but smaller.

Bark: Smooth and gray on young trees, developing shallow interlacing furrows with age.

Fruits: A nearly spherical nut, approximately 1 inch in diameter, with a thin husk with four wings. Husk typically splits at maturity. Often present in large numbers on the ground in winter.

Similar species in winter: Pecan (page 132) and pignut hickory (page 130).

CAROLINA BUCKTHORN

Rhamnaceae
Frangula caroliniana

GENERAL DESCRIPTION

A shrub or small tree, up to 20 feet tall, usually with a short trunk and a spreading crown. Sporadic, but sometimes locally abundant, on moist lower slopes in the Piedmont, usually in the understory of deciduous hardwood forests. Simple alternate leaves are elliptical to oblong, up to 5 inches long, with a very finely serrated or toothed margin.

WINTER ID FEATURES

Twig and leaf scars: Slender, reddish- or grayish-brown, and usually pubescent. Small crescent-shaped leaf scars contain many visible bundle scars. Twig has an unpleasant smell, similar to a ladybug, when crushed or scratched.

Buds: Terminal buds naked, up to 0.25 inch long, and covered with dense tan pubescence. Lateral buds much smaller or often absent.

Bark: Grayish-brown, with prominent lenticels and numerous light and dark colored patches. Shallow furrows sometimes developing with age.

Fruits: A pea-sized drupe, red in color, maturing in summer and generally not present in the wintertime.

Similar species in winter: Pawpaw (page 94).

HAZEL ALDER

Betulaceae
Alnus serrulata

GENERAL DESCRIPTION

A small tree or large shrub (typically less than 30 feet tall), often with multiple erect but twisted stems. Common in wetlands, bogs, and riparian zones that receive ample sunlight, both in the Piedmont and mountains. Elliptical leaves are 2–4 inches long with a finely serrated margin, dark green and slightly lustrous above, lighter green with some pubescence below.

WINTER ID FEATURES

Twig and leaf scars: Slender, reddish-brown, with a grayish pubescence. Small leaf scars.

Buds: Terminal and lateral buds have valvate reddish-purple scales (generally two, sometimes three) and are stalked.

Bark: Thin and grayish-brown, sometimes with a splotchy appearance. Distinctive fluting.

Fruits: Male and female catkins present on the same tree and persist through the winter. Male catkins are up to 1.5 inches long; female catkins are shorter (rarely more than 0.5 inch) and rounder, resembling a small pine cone.

Similar species in winter: American hornbeam (page 154), hazelnut (page 156), and witchhazel (page 100).

YELLOW-POPLAR

Magnoliaceae
Liriodendron tulipifera

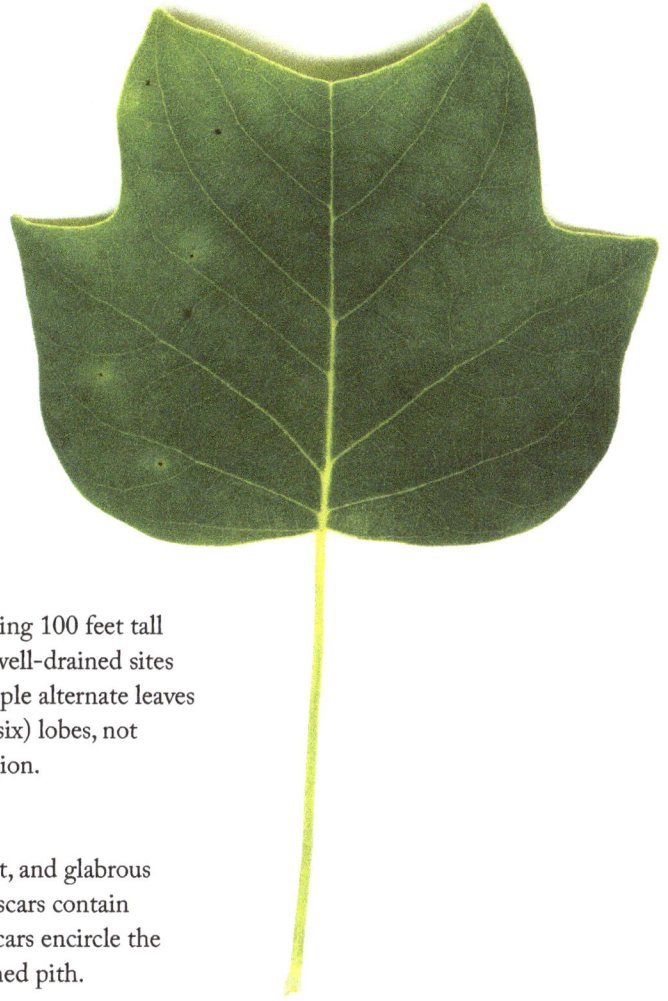

GENERAL DESCRIPTION

A large, sometimes massive tree, often exceeding 100 feet tall and 3–4 feet in diameter. Frequent in moist, well-drained sites such as protected coves and lower slopes. Simple alternate leaves are 5–6 inches across with four (occasionally six) lobes, not resembling any other native species in the region.

WINTER ID FEATURES

Twig and leaf scars: Reddish-brown, stout, and glabrous (sometimes lustrous). Large circular leaf scars contain numerous visible bundle scars. Stipular scars encircle the twig right above the leaf scar. Diaphragmed pith.

Buds: Terminal buds are large (up to 0.5 inch long) with two valvate scales resembling praying hands or a duck's bill. Scale color changes from green to purplish-brown as winter progresses. Lateral buds similar but smaller.

Bark: Gray and smooth on small trees, with distinctive inverted V-shaped marks at each branch. Thick furrows develop with age.

Fruits: An upright, cone-like aggregate of samaras, up to 2.5 inches long. Fruits mature in late summer and early fall, at which point they open and disperse the seeds.

Similar species in winter: Cucumber magnolia (page 142) and eastern cottonwood (page 82).

DEVIL'S WALKINGSTICK

Araliaceae
Aralia spinosa

GENERAL DESCRIPTION

A thicket-forming shrub or small tree (occasionally **exceeding** 25 feet tall) with a broad, spreading crown. Found in **moist** sites and forest edges in the Piedmont and in lower **elevation** mountains. Distinctive alternate bi- or tripinnately **compound** leaves, up to 4 feet long, are a unique feature.

WINTER ID FEATURES

Twig and leaf scars: Very stout, light grayish-brown **or brown** in color, with abundant sharp prickles, especially around the leaf scars. Orange lenticels. Triangular leaf scar wraps almost completely around the twig.

Buds: Terminal buds are large, blunt-tipped, with valvate scales. Lateral buds similar, but smaller and appressed.

Bark: Brown and thin, with abundant prickles. Shallow furrows developing with age.

Fruits: Abundant dark purple drupes, in large red branching panicles at the top of the stem. Fruits mature in fall, but often persist through the winter.

Similar species in winter: None.

HONEYLOCUST

Fabaceae
Gleditsia tricanthos

GENERAL DESCRIPTION

A medium-sized tree, approaching 80 feet tall, but usually smaller. Occasionally found in moist areas along streams, forest edges, fencerows and old fields in the Piedmont and low- to mid-elevation mountains. Foliage is unique in that pinnately compound and bipinnately compound leaves are found on the same tree.

WINTER ID FEATURES

Twig and leaf scars: Typically stout, lustrous and brown or reddish-brown in color. Lenticels readily visible. Clusters of extremely sharp, branched thorns often present. Leaf scars U shaped, with prominent bundle scars within.

Buds: Buds are tiny, round, brownish, and mostly hidden by the leaf scar.

Bark: Gray and smooth on small trees, developing large, scaly, sometimes curly, plates with age.

Fruits: Distinctive large legume, usually 6–10 inches long, sometimes larger. Green when young, becoming dark brown or black and twisted in winter. Often persistent in winter.

Similar species in winter: Black locust (page 114) and mimosa (page 126).

BLACK LOCUST
Fabaceae
Robinia pseudoacacia

GENERAL DESCRIPTION

A medium-sized tree, up to 60 feet tall (occasionally larger),
usually with a crooked trunk and irregular crown. Typically
occurs on drier upper slopes in the mountains, but occasionally
found on lower slopes, field margins, and clearcuts. Through
planting and range expansion, it is now commonly found
throughout the Piedmont. Pinnately compound alternate leaves
are up to 15 inches long, with elliptical pale green leaflets.

WINTER ID FEATURES

Twig and leaf scars: Twigs are dark brown to nearly black,
zigzag in shape, angular in cross-section, and often have a
pair of stout stipular spines at each node. Leaf scars are large
and raised.

Buds: Terminal buds absent; lateral buds hidden within the
leaf scar and scarcely visible.

Bark: Gray with shallow furrows when young, becoming
thicker, darker, and with very deep interlacing furrows with
age.

Fruits: A flattened, papery legume, up to 4 inches long,
similar to eastern redbud. Fruits contain up to 12 flattened
reddish-brown seeds.

Similar species in winter: Honeylocust (page 112) and
mimosa (page 126).

OSAGE-ORANGE
Moraceae
Maclura pomifera

GENERAL DESCRIPTION

A medium-sized tree, up to 50 feet tall and 18 inches in diameter, usually with a short trunk and an irregular crown. Not native to the Piedmont or mountains, but occasionally planted around homesites and fencerows. Simple and alternate leaves are ovate to lanceolate in shape, glabrous and slightly lustrous, with entire margins.

WINTER ID FEATURES

Twig and leaf scars: Fairly stout and zigzag, somewhat triangular in cross-section, gray to orangeish-brown in color. Spur shoots (twigs with very short internodes) often present. Release a sticky, milky sap when cut. Extremely stout and sharp thorns above a small semicircular leaf scar.

Buds: Small, round and brownish, usually with five imbricate bud scales. Scale features not easily visible without a hand lens.

Bark: Orangeish-brown and scaly when young, becoming increasingly brown deep irregular furrows with age.

Fruits: A large, firm, spherical multiple (clump) of drupes, up to 5 inches in diameter. Yellow when fresh, turning brown after falling. Exudes a milky, citrusy sap when cut or broken. Decaying fruits are often found below the tree in the winter.

Similar species in winter: Red mulberry (page 76).

HAWTHORN

Rosaceae
Crataegus spp.

GENERAL DESCRIPTION

A shrub or small tree, typically less than 10 feet tall, usually with multiple stems and a twisted, scraggly appearance. Found on a wide variety of upland sites, in both the Piedmont and mountains. There are several species in the region, and they can be difficult to distinguish from one another due to hybridization and within-species variability. Simple and alternate leaves are often teardrop shaped, serrated, and sometimes with small lobes.

WINTER ID FEATURES

Twig and leaf scars: Slender and zigzag, usually glabrous and sometimes lustrous, and often armed with extremely sharp unbranched thorns. Leaf scars are very small.

Buds: Buds are very small and usually round.

Bark: Smooth and gray, brown or grayish-brown when small, sometimes scaly on larger individuals.

Fruits: Small pomes (usually less than 0.5 inch across), similar to an apple, containing up to five seeds. Fruits mature in the fall and sometimes persist into winter are not eaten by animals.

Similar species in winter: Callery pear (page 80) and tree sparkleberry (page 164).

SWEETGUM

Altingiaceae
Liquidambar styraciflua

GENERAL DESCRIPTION

A large tree, occasionally exceeding 100 feet tall and 3 feet in diameter. Found across a range of sites—from moist alluvial soils, where it grows the largest, to drier upland sites. A rapid colonizer of disturbed sites due to its prolific seeding ability. Unique star-shaped palmately compound alternate foliage, usually with five serrated lobes, distinguishes it from most other native species in the region.

WINTER ID FEATURES

Twig and leaf scars: Slender to stout, green, brown, or greenish-brown and often lustrous. Light-colored lenticels prominent. Sometimes has corky ridges, especially on young trees. Leaf scars are crescent shaped with three light-colored bundle scars within.

Buds: Terminal buds have lustrous brown and green bud scales, up to 0.375 inches long, becoming nearly black in late winter. Lateral buds similar but smaller.

Bark: Gray or grayish-brown, developing shallow furrows with age.

Fruits: A distinctive spiny ball of capsules, up to 1.5 inches in diameter, changing from green to brown at maturity. Fruits often persist on the tree during the winter and can be abundant on the ground.

Similar species in winter: Eastern cottonwood (page 82), winged elm (page 184), and blackgum (page 72).

WINGED SUMAC

Anacardiaceae
Rhus copallinum

GENERAL DESCRIPTION

A multistemmed shrub or small tree, occasionally to 20 feet tall, often forming dense thickets. Commonly found in the Piedmont and mountains along roadsides, powerline right-of-ways, and field margins, where there is abundant sunlight. Pinnately compound alternate leaves are up to 12 inches long, with up to 15 lanceolate leaflets and a distinctive wing on the rachis.

WINTER ID FEATURES

Twig and leaf scars: Moderately stout, blunt-tipped, reddish-brown, and pubescent, covered with corky lenticels and fine pubescence. Leaf scars are U shaped. Twig exudes a sticky sap when cut.

Buds: Terminal buds are absent; lateral buds are small, round, naked, and densely pubescent—partially surrounded by the leaf scar.

Bark: Reddish- or grayish-brown and thin, with prominent lenticels on younger stems. Larger stems may develop a scaly appearance.

Fruits: Clusters of small (0.125 inch) reddish-brown drupes, similar to smooth sumac. Fruits mature in the fall but frequently persist into the winter.

Similar species in winter: Smooth sumac (page 124).

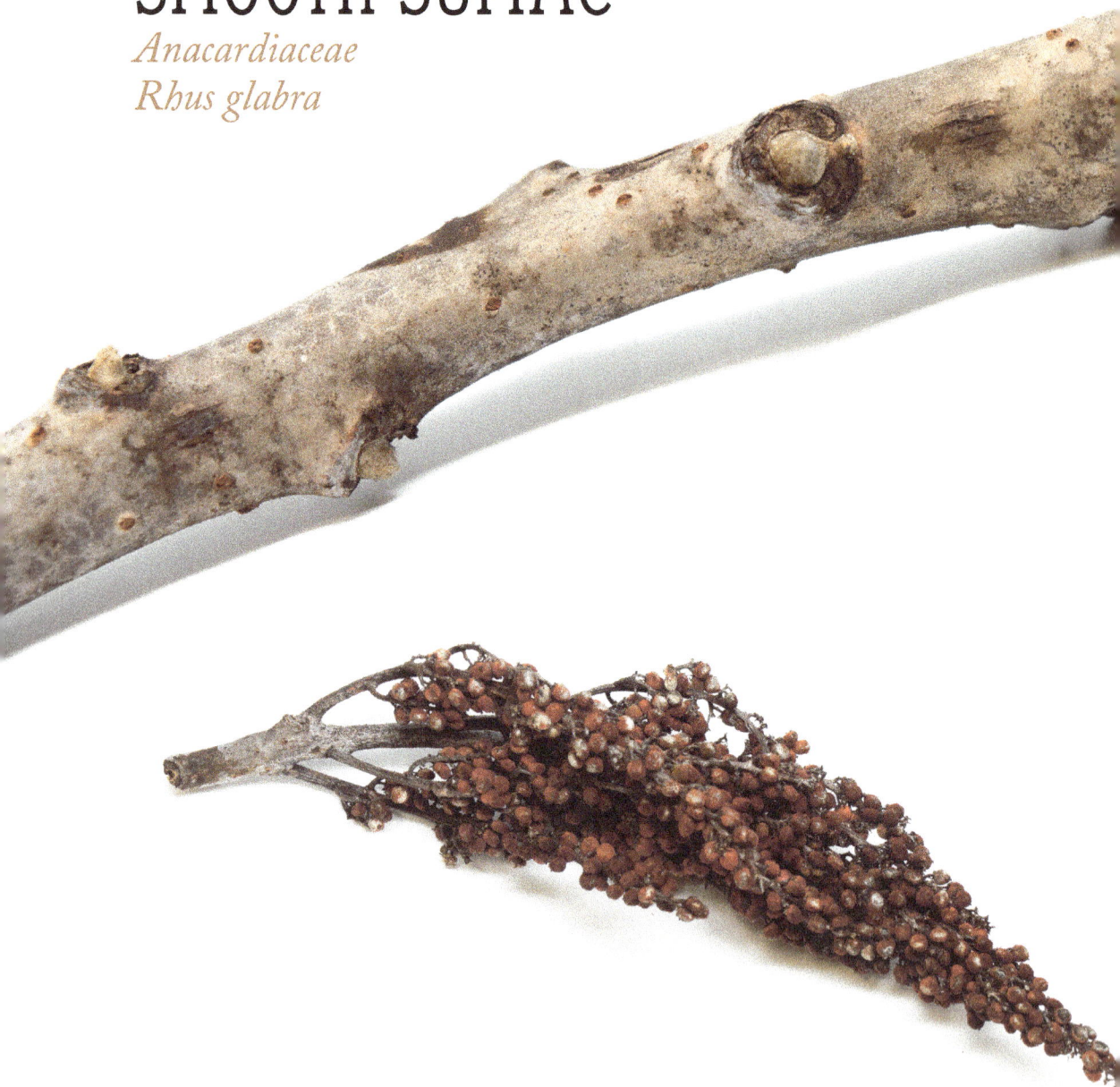

SMOOTH SUMAC
Anacardiaceae
Rhus glabra

GENERAL DESCRIPTION

A multistemmed shrub or small tree, occasionally to 20 feet tall, often forming dense thickets. Commonly found in the Piedmont and mountains along roadsides, powerline right-of-ways, and field margins, where there is abundant sunlight. More common in the mountains than winged sumac. Pinnately compound alternate leaves are up to 24 inches long, with up to 27 serrated lanceolate leaflets (usually less) that are glaucous on the underside.

WINTER ID FEATURES

Twig and leaf scars: Stout, blunt-tipped, grayish-brown, and glaucous, covered with corky lenticels. Leaf scars are horseshoe shaped. Twig exudes a sticky sap when cut.

Buds: Terminal buds are absent; lateral buds are small, round, naked, and covered with a light tan or silvery pubescence—partially surrounded by the leaf scar.

Bark: Brown and thin, with prominent lenticels on younger stems. Larger stems may develop a scaly appearance.

Fruits: Clusters of small (0.125inch) bright red drupes. Fruits mature in the fall but frequently persist into the winter.

Similar species in winter: Winged sumac (page 122).

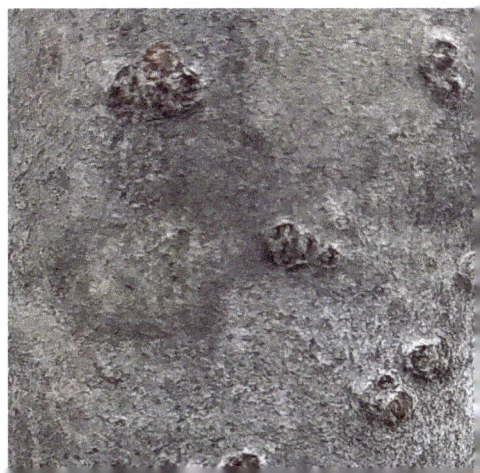

MIMOSA

Fabaceae
Albizia julibrissin

GENERAL DESCRIPTION

A small nonnative tree (typically less than 30 feet tall), usually with a short trunk and broad, spreading branches. A nonnative species, mimosa is commonly found in disturbed sites, and along roadsides and fencerows. Bipinnately compound leaves approach 18–20 inches long.

WINTER ID FEATURES

Twig and leaf scars: Twigs are green to black with a zigzag appearance. Lenticels prominent. Leaf scar has three rounded lobes. Small stipular spines occasionally present.

Buds: Terminal bud absent. Small reddish-brown buds have few scales and are nestled between the upper two lobes of the leaf scar.

Bark: Smooth and gray or grayish-brown. Texture and color change little with age.

Fruits: A flattened, papery legume, 5–6 inches long, grayish-brown in winter, containing several dark brown seeds.

Similar species in winter: Black locust (page 114), honeylocust (page 112), and eastern redbud (page 166).

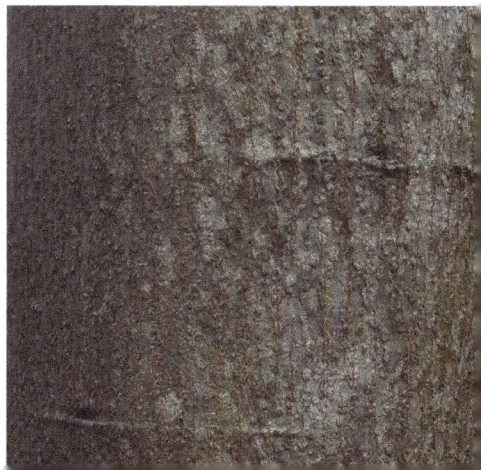

KENTUCKY COFFEETREE

Fabaceae
Gymnocladus dioicus

GENERAL DESCRIPTION

A medium- to large-sized tree, up to 90 feet tall and 2 feet in diameter. Occurs in in fertile, moist sites, including bottomlands, generally in the Midwest, but is occasionally planted as a landscape tree and has become naturalized in the Piedmont and mountains. Leaves are large (up to 3 feet long) and are typically once-pinnately compound toward the base, becoming bipinnately compound toward the tip. Leaflets are ovate in shape, up to 2.5 inches long, and typically fall off in early to mid-fall, before the petiole abscises from the twig.

WINTER ID FEATURES

Twig and leaf scars: Stout, crooked, and grayish-brown in color. Leaf scars large and heart shaped or three-lobed leaf scar, with abundant large bundle scars within. A cut twig reveals a distinctive rust-colored pith.

Buds: Terminal bud generally absent. Lateral buds are small (less than 0.25 inch across), round, and slightly sunken into the top of the leaf scar.

Bark: Gray or slightly grayish-brown, developing flat scaly ridges that curl outward on one side.

Fruits: A reddish-brown legume pod, becoming nearly black with age, up to 8 inches long. Fruits contain up to five black seeds, ripen in summer, and often persist into the winter.

Similar species in winter: Tree-of-heaven (page 152) and Chinaberry (page 150).

PIGNUT HICKORY

Juglandaceae
Carya glabra

GENERAL DESCRIPTION

A stout, large tree, often approaching 80 feet tall. Common in well-drained upland sites, and occasionally moist sites, in the Piedmont and low- to mid-elevation mountains. Pinnately compound, alternate leaves have five to seven leaflets. Leaflets, petiole, and rachis are glabrous. Note that red hickory, which is sometimes considered a variety of pignut hickory (*Carya glabra* var. *odorata*), is essentially identical to pignut hickory, differing only in bark characteristics.

WINTER ID FEATURES

Twig and leaf scars: Fairly stout (but less so than other hickories), dark colored, and glabrous. Leaf scars large and three lobed or heart shaped, with abundant, readily visible bundle scars within.

Buds: Terminal bud is somewhat pointed, fairly large (up to 0.375 inches in diameter), with dark brown imbricate scales. Lateral buds similar but smaller.

Red Hickory

Bark: Smooth when young, becoming darker with interlacing ridges with age. Ridges are not as large as those of mockernut hickory. Red hickory bark has a much shaggier texture.

Fruits: Large spherical or pear-shaped nuts, up to 1.25 inches in diameter, with a thin wingless husk. Often abundant on the ground in late fall and winter.

Similar species in winter: Bitternut hickory (page 102), mockernut hickory (page 136), red hickory (this page), and shagbark hickory (page 134).

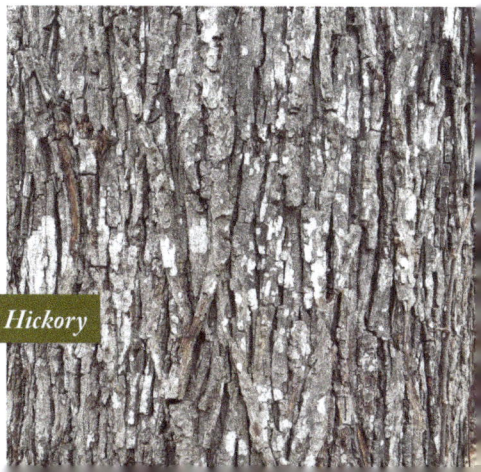

Pignut Hickory

PECAN
Juglandaceae
Carya illinoinensis

GENERAL DESCRIPTION

A sometimes massive tree, capable of growing well over 100 feet tall (usually less). Native to the Mississippi valley and westward, but commonly around homesites and farms, especially in the Piedmont. Pinnately compound, alternate leaves have nine to 17 finely serrated pubescent leaflets.

WINTER ID FEATURES

Twig and leaf scars: Fairly stout, light brown, with fine pubescence near the tip. Leaf scars large and three lobed, with abundant, readily visible bundle scars within.

Buds: Terminal bud is pointed, often beaked, fairly large (up to 0.5 inch long), with brown imbricate scales. Lateral buds similar but smaller and rounder.

Bark: Smooth when young, becoming darker and developing narrow, sometimes shaggy or scaly ridges.

Fruits: Large football shaped nuts, up 2 inches long, with a slightly winged husk.

Similar species in winter: Bitternut hickory (page 102) and butternut (page 138).

SHAGBARK HICKORY

Juglandaceae
Carya ovata

GENERAL DESCRIPTION

A large tree, sometimes exceeding 100 feet tall. Occasional in moist alluvial soils and lower slopes and limestone outcrops. Pinnately compound, alternate leaves typically have five leaflets. Leaflets, petiole rachis are usually glabrous, but sometimes have a fine pubescence. Fine ciliate hairs, barely visible, line the serrated leaf margins.

WINTER ID FEATURES

Twig and leaf scars: Stout and tomentose, particularly toward the tip. Three-lobed leaf scar, similar to other hickories.

Buds: Terminal bud is somewhat pointed, large (up to 0.75 inches long), with three to four brown imbricate scales. Lateral buds similar but smaller.

Bark: Smooth and gray when young, developing broad, shaggy, exfoliating plates with age.

Fruits: Large nuts, up to 2 inches in diameter, with a thick (up to 0.375 inch) husk. Husk similar to mockernut hickory, but lighter colored on the inside. Often abundant on the ground in late fall and winter.

Similar species in winter: Mockernut hickory (page 136), pignut hickory (page 130), and red hickory (see pignut hickory).

MOCKERNUT HICKORY
Juglandaceae
Carya tomentosa

GENERAL DESCRIPTION

A stout, large tree, often approaching 100 feet tall. Common in well-drained upland sites in the Piedmont and low- to mid-elevation mountains. Pinnately compound, alternate leaves typically have seven leaflets. Coarse woolly tomentum is present on the underside of the leaflets, as well as the petiole and rachis.

WINTER ID FEATURES

Twig and leaf scars: Stout, often with pubescence near the tip. Leaf scars large and three lobed, with abundant, readily visible bundle scars within.

Buds: Terminal bud is large, rounded (up to 0.75 inch in diameter), with light tan-colored imbricate scales. Lateral buds similar but smaller.

Bark: Gray with shallow furrows on young trees, becoming darker with coarse interlacing ridges with age.

Fruits: Large nuts, up to 2 inches in diameter, with a thick (up to 0.375 inch) husk. Often abundant on the ground in late fall and winter.

Similar species in winter: Pignut hickory (page 130) and shagbark hickory (page 134).

BUTTERNUT

Juglandaceae
Juglans cinerea

GENERAL DESCRIPTION

A medium-sized tree, rarely exceeding 70 feet tall, similar
in form to black walnut but generally smaller. An occasional
component of mixed-hardwood forests in moist, well-drained
sites, sometimes along streams. Also found on drier soils of
limestone origin. Pinnately compound, alternate leaves are up to
18 inches long and have up to 17 leaflets. Unlike black walnut,
the terminal leaflet is usually present. Large trees are rare due to
butternut canker, a fungal disease that severely impacts butternut
trees.

WINTER ID FEATURES

Twig and leaf scars: Stout, reddish- or grayish-brown and
glabrous, often with prominent lenticels, with distinctive
U-shaped bundle scars in each lobe of the three-lobed leaf
scar. Typically has a small tuft of hair at the top of the leaf
scar. Chambered pith.

Buds: Terminal buds are light brown, up to 0.375 inches
long, with a few slightly pubescent imbricate scales. Lateral
buds similar but smaller.

Bark: Light grayish-brown, becoming deeply furrowed and
darker (but not as dark as black walnut) with age. Interlacing
ridges on the bark resemble hickories and black walnut.

Fruits: A large oblong nut with an indehiscent
(nonsplitting) husk, similar in size and shape to pecan. Husk
turns from green to brown when mature.

Similar species in winter: Black walnut (page 140), tree-of-
heaven (page 152), and pecan (page 132).

BLACK WALNUT

Juglandaceae
Juglans nigra

GENERAL DESCRIPTION

A large tree often approaching 100 feet tall and 3 feet in
diameter, with stout ascending branches. An occasional
component of mixed-hardwood forests in moist, well-drained
sites. Also frequently found around old homesites and farms.
Pinnately compound, alternate leaves are up to 2 feet long and
have up to 21 leaflets, although the terminal leaflet is usually
short-lived.

WINTER ID FEATURES

Twig and leaf scars: Stout, brown and glabrous, with
prominent bundle scars in each lobe of the three-lobed leaf
scar. Chambered pith.

Buds: Terminal buds are light brown, up to 0.375 inches
long, with a few slightly pubescent imbricate scales. Lateral
buds similar but smaller.

Bark: Dark grayish-brown, becoming deeply furrowed
and almost black with age. Interlacing ridges on the bark
resemble mockernut hickory.

Fruits: A large almost black spherical nut housed within a
thick indehiscent husk, up to 2.5 inches in diameter. Husk
turns from green to brown when mature.

Similar species in winter: Butternut (page 138) and tree-of-
heaven (page 152).

CUCUMBER MAGNOLIA
Magnoliaceae
Magnolia acuminata

GENERAL DESCRIPTION

A large tree, occasionally exceeding 80 feet tall. Found in the overstory of mixed-hardwood forests in the Piedmont and low- and mid-elevation mountains, particularly on north facing slopes and in moist coves. Simple alternate leaves are elliptical in shape and 6–10 inches long. Growth form and bark strongly resemble that of yellow-poplar.

WINTER ID FEATURES

Twig and leaf scars: Stout and reddish-brown, with a stipular scar encircling the twig right above the leaf scar.

Buds: Terminal buds are up to 0.625 inches long, covered with silky pubescence. Lateral buds similar, but smaller.

Bark: Grayish-brown with yellow-poplar-like furrows and ridges developing with age.

Fruits: A small (less than 3 inch) aggregate of follicles, usually curved, containing bright red seeds. Fruit resembles a small cucumber in shape and turns from green to brown with maturity.

Similar species in winter: Bigleaf magnolia (page 146) and yellow-poplar (page 108).

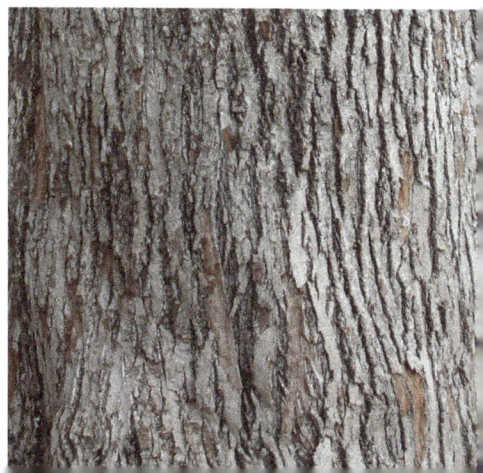

FRASER MAGNOLIA

Magnoliaceae
Magnolia fraseri

GENERAL DESCRIPTION

A small- to medium-sized tree, occasionally exceeding 60 feet tall. Found in the understory and midstory of mixed-hardwood forests in the southern Appalachians, particularly in moist coves. Simple alternate leaves are up to 12 inches long, with two distinctive lobes at the leaf base. Often has multiple trunks.

WINTER ID FEATURES

Twig and leaf scars: Stout and grayish-brown or purplish-brown, with large, half-circular leaf scars.

Buds: Terminal buds are up to 1 inch long and somewhat curved, turning from green to purplish-brown with age.

Bark: Thin, smooth, and grayish-brown when young. Sometimes with dark- and light-colored splotches. Thin scaly plates usually developing on the largest trees.

Fruits: A bright red aggregate of follicles, up to 4 inches long, containing red seeds. Fruit turns dark brown before falling off in winter.

Similar species in winter: Bigleaf magnolia (page 146) and umbrella magnolia (page 148).

BIGLEAF MAGNOLIA
Magnoliaceae
Magnolia macrophylla

GENERAL DESCRIPTION

A small- to medium-sized tree, up to 50 feet tall and 1 foot in diameter. Occurs in moist coves and ravines, most commonly in the Coastal Plain, but also sporadically in the Piedmont and mountains. Simple alternate leaves are oblong in shape, sometimes exceeding 30 inches long and 10 inches wide, with a rounded or heart-shaped base.

WINTER ID FEATURES

Twig and leaf scars: Stout, brittle, and brown, with a rounded, slightly heart-shaped leaf scar. Stipular scar encircles the twig. Some pubescence on the twig, particularly toward the end.

Buds: Large terminal buds (up to 1 inch long) covered in dense silvery white pubescence. Buds sometimes have a curved or hooked appearance.

Bark: Gray or light grayish-brown and smooth, sometimes with small scaly plates on large tree.

Fruits: A nearly spherical cone-like aggregate of follicles, up to 3 inches across, containing bright red seeds.

Similar species in winter: Cucumber magnolia (page 142), Fraser magnolia (page 144), and umbrella magnolia (page 148).

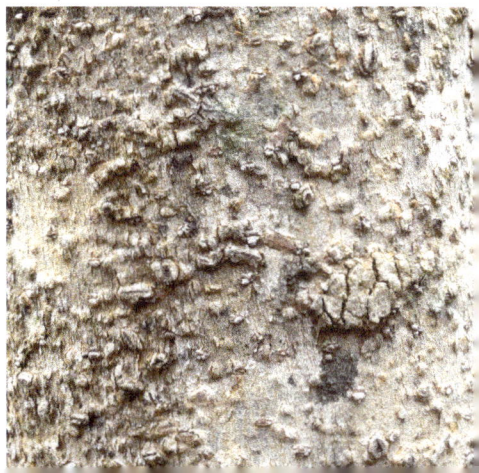

UMBRELLA MAGNOLIA
Magnoliaceae
Magnolia tripetala

GENERAL DESCRIPTION

A small- to medium-sized tree, up to 40 feet tall and 14 inches
in diameter, usually with a short trunk or many stems, and a
broad, spreading crown. Sporadically found in the moist sites
in the Piedmont and in low elevation mountains. Simple and
alternate leaves are large (up to 24 inches long), obovate in
shape, light green above and pale below. Leaf base is narrow and
unlobed, which helps to distinguish it from Fraser magnolia and
bigleaf magnolia.

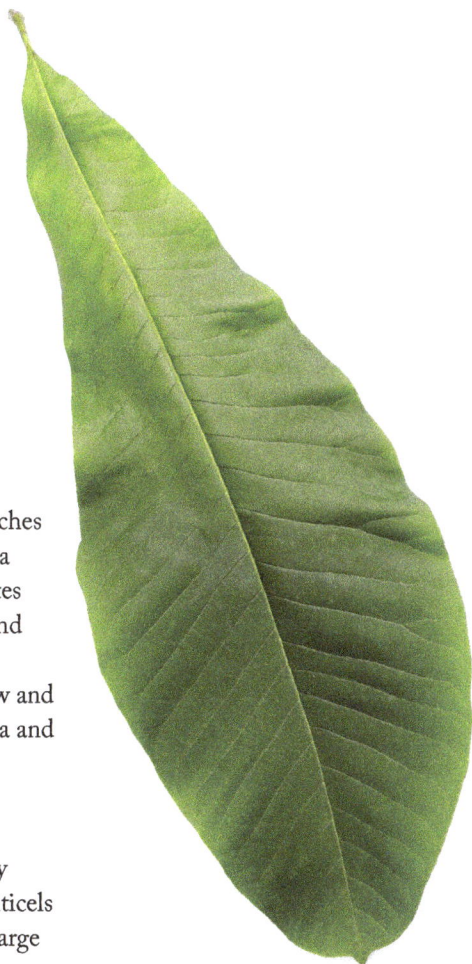

WINTER ID FEATURES

Twig and leaf scars: Stout but easily breakable, typically
greenish-brown or brown in the winter. Prominent lenticels
usually present. Leaf scars are large and circular, with large
bundle scars often visible.

Buds: Terminal buds large (up to 1 inch long), greenish-
purple to purple in the winter, and lacking hairs. Buds
sometimes have a slightly glaucous appearance.

Bark: Thin, smooth and gray, like other magnolias, often
with prominent large lenticels. Shallow furrows sometimes
develop with age.

Fruits: A cone-like aggregate of follicles, similar to other
magnolias, up to 4 inches long, pinkish-red when mature,
turning brown in winter. Fruits contain numerous bright red
seeds.

Similar species in winter: Fraser magnolia (page 144), and
bigleaf magnolia (page 146).

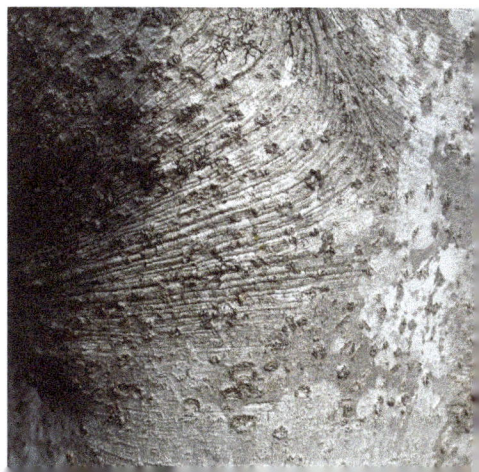

CHINABERRY

Meliaceae
Melia azedarach

GENERAL DESCRIPTION

A small- to medium-sized tree, up to 50 feet tall, with a broad, spreading crown, often with multiple stems. Nonnative and highly invasive, it is common along fencerows and field margins, especially in the Piedmont. Large (up to 2 feet long), bipinnately compound alternate leaves, with lustrous leaflets up to 2 inches long, are distinctive.

WINTER ID FEATURES

Twig and leaf scars: Very stout, greenish-brown to dark brown, with prominent light-colored lenticels. Leaf scars large and three lobed, containing numerous visible bundle scars.

Buds: Buds are small and round, tan to orangeish-brown in color, dense pubescence covering imbricate bud scales, submerged between the top two lobes of the leaf scar.

Bark: Grayish-brown to reddish-brown, smooth when young, developing shallow and sometimes interlacing furrows with age.

Fruits: A yellowish-brown drupe, 0.5–0.75 inches across, borne in hanging clusters, persisting through the winter. Fruits are produced in great numbers and are often visible from a distance.

Similar species in winter: Kentucky coffeetree (page 128) and tree-of-heaven (page 152).

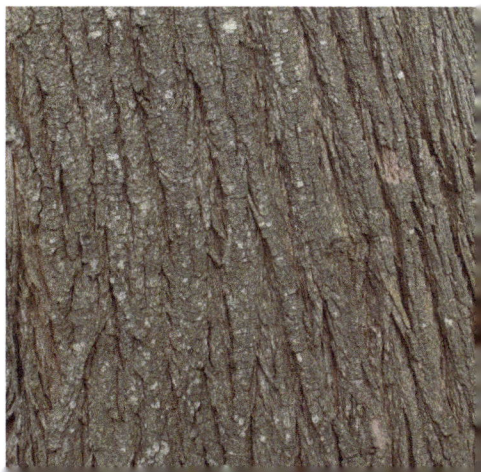

TREE-OF-HEAVEN
Simaroubaceae
Ailanthus altissima

GENERAL DESCRIPTION

A medium-sized nonnative tree, up to 50 feet tall. Commonly found in disturbed sites, and along roadsides, fencerows and rocky areas. Large (1- to 3-foot) pinnately compound leaves have up to 41 leaflets, each with one to two small glands near the base. Glands have the odor of rancid peanut butter.

WINTER ID FEATURES

Twig and leaf scars: Twigs are stout and brittle, with a reddish-brown pith and large heart shaped leaf scars. Bundle scars prominent. Broken twigs share the same smell as the leaves.

Buds: Terminal bud absent. Small reddish-brown buds are partially surrounded by the leaf scar.

Bark: Light brown or gray, often with a mottled "chain mail" appearance, especially on larger trees.

Fruits: A flattened, twisted samara, less than 2 inches long, with a single seed in the center. Matures in the summer, sometimes persisting into the winter.

Similar species in winter: Black walnut (page 140), Chinaberry (page 150), Kentucky coffeetree (page 128), and butternut (page 138).

AMERICAN HORNBEAM

Betulaceae
Carpinus caroliniana

GENERAL DESCRIPTION

A shrub or small tree, rarely more than 30 feet tall. A common understory species in moist sites such as streamsides, coves, and protected lower slopes. Simple alternate leaves are elliptical in shape, typically under 4 inches long, with a doubly serrate margin

WINTER ID FEATURES

Twig and leaf scars: Slender, zigzag twigs, ranging in color from brown, to gray, to reddish-brown. Lenticels faintly visible. Crescent-shaped leaf scars.

Buds: Sharply pointed buds have dark brown and tan imbricate scales, resembling snake scales. Tan color is actually a fine pubescence along the scale margin.

Bark: Bluish-gray and smooth, sometimes splotchy, with distinctive fluting.

Fruits: Small nutlets, below a three-lobed leaf-like bract. Sometimes present in late fall and early winter.

Similar species in winter: Hazel alder (page 106) and eastern hophornbeam (page 158).

HAZELNUT
Betulaceae
Corylus americana

GENERAL DESCRIPTION

A multistemmed shrub, up to 15 feet tall, often forming dense thickets. Found in fertile moist soils, typically below oaks, hickories and other hardwoods, in both the Piedmont and mountains. Hazelnut is not particularly common in the region, but can be locally abundant in some areas. Simple and alternate leaves are roughly elliptical in shape, with a doubly serrated margin and a rounded or heart-shaped base.

WINTER ID FEATURES

Twig and leaf scars: Slender, grayish-brown and zigzag, usually with short, stiff hairs on recent growth. Leaf scars are very small. Male catkins, up to 1 inch long, are sometimes present.

Buds: Terminal buds are up to 0.125 inch long, with a few brown imbricate bud scales. Lateral buds similar to terminals.

Bark: Gray or grayish-brown and smooth when young, larger stems sometimes have a little bit of texture.

Fruits: Hard brown nuts, up to 0.5 inch across, enclosed by two thick, leaf-like bracts with ragged edges. Fruits mature in summer and occasionally persist into winter.

Similar species in winter: Hazel alder (page 106).

EASTERN HOPHORNBEAM

Betulaceae
Ostrya virginiana

GENERAL DESCRIPTION

A small tree, occasionally up to 50 feet tall, often with a short trunk and rounded crown. Occurs sporadically in the Piedmont and mountains, across a range of sites—from drier ridges to floodplain margins. Simple alternate leaves are 3–5 inches long, elliptical to somewhat lanceolate in shape, with a doubly serrate margin. Fine pubescence on the underside of the leaf, especially the veins.

WINTER ID FEATURES

Twig and leaf scars: Slender and reddish-brown, slightly zigzag in appearance, usually glabrous but sometimes has a fine pubescence. Leaf scars very small and can be crescent shaped, half circular, or oval.

Buds: Buds are small and pointed, covered with variegated green and reddish-brown (typically mostly reddish-brown in winter) imbricate bud scales. Small, pointed, preformed catkin (flower) buds sometimes present at the end of the twig.

Bark: Smooth and reddish-brown when young, often with prominent lenticels, developing a distinctive shredded appearance with age.

Fruits: A distinctive hop-like cluster of small nutlets (less than 0.25 inch across) encased in a pubescent, papery sacks.

Similar species in winter: American hornbeam (page 154), black birch (page 68), and yellow birch (page 66).

COMMON PERSIMMON

Ebenaceae
Diospyros virginiana

GENERAL DESCRIPTION

A small- to medium-sized tree, sometimes approaching 70 feet tall. Common across a range of sites, from dry to moist, and frequently a thicket-forming pioneer species on disturbed sites. Simple alternate leaves oval to elliptical in shape, 2–5 inches long, with entire margins and pointed tips.

WINTER ID FEATURES

Twig and leaf scars: Slender sometimes zigzag in appearance, with orange lenticels, and occasional pubescence (usually glabrous). Raised, leaf scars are broadly crescent or shield shaped.

Buds: Lacks a true terminal bud. Laterals are small, triangular and dark (nearly black) and composed of two overlapping scales.

Bark: Grayish-brown and fairly smooth when young, developing thick, nearly black, square plates with age.

Fruits: A large berry, approaching 2 inches in diameter. Green in early fall, becoming orangeish-red or nearly purple after frost. Rarely persistent due to consumption by wildlife.

Similar species in winter: Blackgum (page 72), Carolina silverbell (page 180), rusty blackhaw (page 24), flowering dogwood (page 26), and Sourwood (page 162).

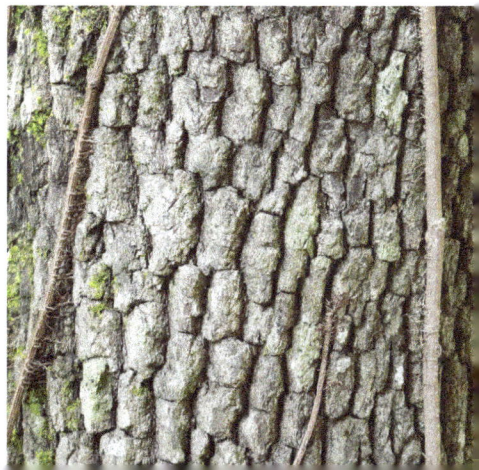

SOURWOOD

Ericaceae
Oxydendrum arboreum

GENERAL DESCRIPTION

A medium-sized tree, up to 60 feet tall, often multi-stemmed with bent or twisted trunks, with an irregularly shaped crown. Common across the Piedmont and low- to mid-elevation mountains, particularly in drier mixed-hardwood forests. Simple and alternate leaves are elliptical to lanceolate in shape, 4–7 inches long, with a finely serrated margin.

WINTER ID FEATURES

Twig and leaf scars: Moderately slender, green to red (predominantly red in winter), slightly zigzag, with prominent lenticels. Leaf scars very small, half circular, and slightly elevated.

Buds: Buds are very small and round. Scales are almost invisible to the naked eye.

Bark: Dull and slate gray in color, with a small amount of brown or reddish-brown sometimes visible. On larger trees, ridges develop a distinctive rectangular blocky appearance.

Fruits: Small brown capsules, about 0.25 inch long, clustered on drooping stalks. Fruits often persist on the tree into the winter, or can be found in abundance on the ground.

Similar species in winter: Blackgum (page 72), Carolina silverbell (page 180), common persimmon (page 160), and sassafras (page 172).

TREE SPARKLEBERRY

Ericaceae
Vaccinium arboreum

GENERAL DESCRIPTION

A multistemmed shrub, occasionally a tree up to 25 feet tall, with crooked branches and often with a Bonsai-like appearance. The largest native blueberry in the Piedmont and low-elevation mountains, it is primarily found in dry sites below yellow pines or mixed hardwoods. Simple and alternate leaves are elliptical in shape, up to 2 inches long, very lustrous on top, and tardily deciduous.

WINTER ID FEATURES

Twig and leaf scars: Very slender and zigzag, reddish- or grayish-brown, with small, half-circular leaf scars containing a single bundle scar.

Buds: Buds are very small and round, with details not clearly visible without a hand lens.

Bark: Thin gray outer bark, exfoliating to reveal a distinctive reddish-brown inner bark.

Fruits: A small lustrous black berry, up to 0.25 inch across. Fruits mature in the fall and occasionally persist into early winter.

Similar species in winter: Hawthorn (page 118).

EASTERN REDBUD

Fabaceae
Cercis canadensis

GENERAL DESCRIPTION

A shrub or small tree, rarely exceeding 30 feet. A common understory species, across a range of sites, from moist to dry, in the Piedmont and low-elevation mountains. Simple heart-shaped leaves are 3–5 inches in diameter and usually glabrous. Showy purple or pink flowers emerge before the leaves and can be an excellent identification feature in late winter and early spring.

WINTER ID FEATURES

Twig and leaf scars: Slender and zigzag in appearance, ranging in color from dark reddish-brown to nearly black. Prominent light-colored lenticels throughout. Leaf scars small and half circular or shield shaped.

Buds: Terminal bud is absent. Lateral buds tiny, slightly pointed and appressed. Globose flower buds sometimes present at nodes, often numerous on trees growing in abundant sunlight.

Bark: Smooth and gray or brown when young, often developing thin, scaly plates with age.

Fruits: A papery, flattened legume, dark brown in color, containing several small, flattened black seeds. Occur in clusters on the underside of twigs and branches. Maturing in summer, but persisting through the winter.

Similar species in winter: Mimosa (page 126), yellowwood (page 98), and black locust (page 114).

AMERICAN CHESTNUT

Fagaceae
Castanea dentata

GENERAL DESCRIPTION

Historically one of the largest trees in southern Appalachians and Piedmont, sometimes exceeding 100 feet in height and several feet in diameter. Typically, it was found on ridges and rocky, exposed sites, but grew largest in fertile moist soils. A fungal blight in the early to mid-1900s wiped out nearly all large trees; scattered stump sprouts (generally less than 20 feet tall) are largely what remains today. Simple and alternate leaves are oblong in shape, up to 10 inches long. Leaves are thin and papery, glabrous, with a distinctive dentate margin with outward pointing bristle tips.

WINTER ID FEATURES

Twig and leaf scars: Fairly slender, slightly zigzag, glabrous to lustrous reddish-brown in color with scattered light-colored lenticels. Leaf scars are small and semicircular.

Buds: Buds similar in color to twigs, up to 0.25 inch long, with two or three glabrous imbricate bud scales.

Bark: Smooth and grayish-brown when young, becoming coarser and darker with flattened plates or interlacing hickory-like ridges on larger trees.

Fruits: A large extremely spiny bur, up to 2.5 inches across, containing two to three shiny brown and slightly pubescent nuts. Fruiting trees are rare, as they typically succumb to the blight before reaching reproductive size.

Similar species in winter: Chinese chestnut (page 170).

CHINESE CHESTNUT

Fagaceae
Castanea mollissima

GENERAL DESCRIPTION

Similar to American chestnut, but smaller at maturity, with a short trunk and broad, spreading crown. Planted widely across the in the 20th century due to its resistance to the chestnut blight. Often found around old homesites. Simple and alternate leaves are similar to American chestnut, but thicker, with pubescence on the underside, and with a less pronounced dentate margin.

WINTER ID FEATURES

Twig and leaf scars: Fairly slender, slightly zigzag, pubescent and gray or grayish-brown in color with distinctive lenticels. Leaf scars are small and semicircular.

Buds: Gray or grayish-brown, with dense gray pubescence covering two to three imbricate bud scales.

Bark: Gray or grayish-brown, developing deep furrows with age.

Fruits: A large extremely spiny bur, up to 2.5 inches across, containing two to three shiny brown and glabrous to lustrous nuts (lacking the pubescence of American chestnut).

Similar species in winter: American chestnut (page 168).

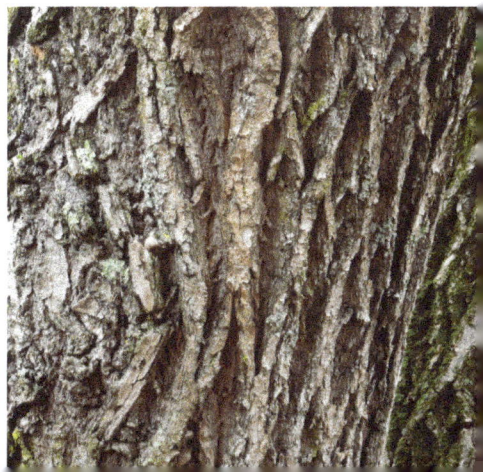

SASSAFRAS
Lauraceae
Sassafras albidum

GENERAL DESCRIPTION

A small tree or shrub, occasionally 50 feet tall, rarely straight, typically with a narrow and flat crown. Common in both the Piedmont and mountains, were it is typically found in forest edges, field margins, or other sites with abundant sunlight. Simple and alternate leaves are 3–6 inches long, and trimorphic; they can be three lobed (like a turkey foot), two lobed (like a mitten), or unlobed, all on the same tree.

WINTER ID FEATURES

Twig and leaf scars: Slender and ranging in color from yellowish-green to orangeish-brown. Leaf scars very small. Twig has a spicy smell when scratched or crushed.

Buds: Terminal buds are large (up to 0.375 inches across) and club like, covered with three to five imbricate scales. Lateral buds much smaller.

Bark: Dark green with splotches of brown scales on small trees, becoming thicker, furrowed, and reddish-brown with age.

Fruits: Lustrous bluish-black drupes, less than 0.5 inch across, with red stalks. Fruits mature in the summer and rarely persist into winter.

Similar species in winter: Sourwood (page 162).

SWEETBAY MAGNOLIA

Magnoliaceae
Magnolia virginiana

GENERAL DESCRIPTION

A large shrub or small tree, typically under 20 feet tall but occasionally larger, often with multiple stems. Primarily limited to acidic, wet sites on the Coastal Plain, but native range extends to the lower Piedmont. Commonly planted as a landscape tree outside of the native range. Simple and alternate leaves are up to 6 inches long, elliptical in shape, are evergreen in warmer climates, but typically deciduous on the colder fringes of its range.

WINTER ID FEATURES

Twig and leaf scars: Much thinner than other magnolias, green to greenish-gray in color, with distinctive stipular scars circling the twig above small leaf scars. Spicy fragrance when crushed.

Buds: Terminal buds long (up to 0.75 inch) and pointed, imbricate scales covered with silky silver hairs. Lateral buds much smaller than terminal buds.

Bark: Thin, smooth and gray, like other magnolias, with shallow furrows sometimes developing with age.

Fruits: A small cone-like aggregate of follicles, up to 2 inches long, reddish-pink when mature, turning reddish-brown in winter. Fruits contain numerous bright red seeds.

Similar species in winter: Horsesugar (page 84).

FIRE CHERRY

Rosaceae
Prunus pensylvanica

GENERAL DESCRIPTION

A small, often multistemmed tree, rarely more than 30 feet tall and 6 inches in diameter, with an irregular crown. In the southern Appalachians, it is only found at high elevations (higher than 4,000 feet), often found on the edges of spruce–fir forests, or mixed with northern hardwoods. Simple alternate leaf is lanceolate in shape, 3–6 inches long, with a rounded base and finely serrated margins.

WINTER ID FEATURES

Twig and leaf scars: Slender, glabrous, lustrous, and red or reddish-brown, with prominent orangeish lenticels. Like many cherry species, glaucous patches may also be present. Small, slightly elevated leaf scars. Like other cherries, has a "skunky" smell when scratched.

Buds: Terminal buds are small (0.125 inch), somewhat pointed, and clustered at the end of the twig. Lateral buds similar, but smaller. Imbricate reddish-brown bud scales have a fine ciliate margin.

Bark: Shiny and reddish-brown with large, raised, horizontal lenticels. On larger trees, bark may become grayer and peel off in papery horizontal strips.

Fruits: A small (0.25 inch) red drupe, hanging individually from short stalks. Fruits mature in the summer and generally do not persist into winter.

Similar species in winter: Black cherry (page 178).

BLACK CHERRY

Rosaceae
Prunus serotina

GENERAL DESCRIPTION

A medium- to large-sized tree, up to 90 feet tall and 2 feet in diameter (usually smaller), often with a long, straight trunk and broad crown. Found on a wide variety of sites in the Piedmont and mountains, from roadsides and forest edges to mixed-hardwood forests. Simple alternate leaves are highly variable in shape, from nearly round to very lanceolate, with fine serrations on the margin.

WINTER ID FEATURES

Twig and leaf scars: Slender and reddish-brown, often glabrous on one side and glaucous on the other. Small, light-colored lenticels usually visible. Small leaf scars. Like other cherries, has a "skunky" smell when scratched.

Buds: Buds are small and covered with numerous reddish-brown imbricate scales, with some green color usually present.

Bark: Bark is silvery-gray and smooth, with prominent lenticels when young. Becoming much darker and scalier on trees larger than 5 inches in diameter.

Fruits: A small drupe, about 0.375 inch in diameter, clustered on hanging stalks. Fruits mature in summer and generally do not persist into winter.

Similar species in winter: Downy serviceberry (page 41) and fire cherry (page 176).

CAROLINA SILVERBELL

Styracaceae
Halesia carolina

GENERAL DESCRIPTION

A small- to medium-sized tree, occasionally approaching 50 feet tall but usually much smaller. Found occasionally in the understory of mixed-hardwood forests in moist sites, often along streams. Simple alternate leaves are 3–6 inches long, ovate in shape, with a finely toothed margin. Fine pubescence usually present on lower leaf surfaces.

WINTER ID FEATURES

Twig and leaf scars: Slender, slightly zigzag, and brown, sometimes shredded and/or with a fine silky pubescence. Leaf scars half circular or slightly crescent shaped, with a single bundle scar.

Buds: Terminal buds are absent. Lateral buds are small and ovoid, with a pointed tip and usually three brown or greenish-brown imbricate bud scales.

Bark: Reddish-brown with white or pale yellow stripes when young, becoming furrowed with orangeish-brown stripes with age.

Fruits: A distinctive four-winged drupe, up to 2 inches long, turning from yellow to brown with age. Fruits often persist through the winter.

Similar species in winter: Common persimmon (page 160) and sourwood (page 162).

SUGARBERRY

Ulmaceae
Celtis laevigata

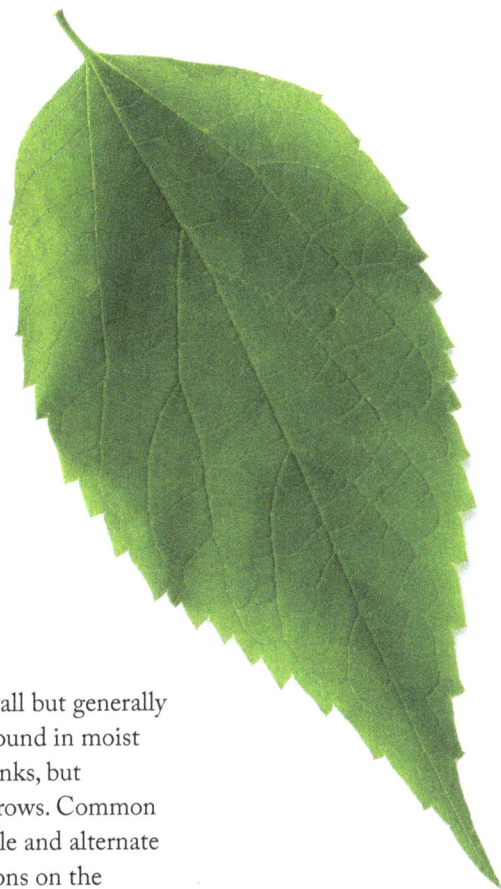

GENERAL DESCRIPTION

A medium-sized tree, occasionally up to 80 feet tall but generally smaller, with a broad, rounded crown. Typically found in moist sites, like lower slopes, floodplains, and stream banks, but occasionally found in open areas and along fencerows. Common in the Piedmont but rare in the mountains. Simple and alternate leaves are up to 5 inches long, with coarse serrations on the upper half. Leaves are often infested with small white woolly aphids, which excrete a sweet honeydew, resulting in plants being covered with a black sooty mold.

WINTER ID FEATURES

Twig and leaf scars: Slender, zigzag, and brown (often black when covered with mold), with small light colored lenticels. Leaf scars are half circular.

Buds: Terminal buds are absent, but a unique false terminal—when present—is hooked at a 90-degree angle. Lateral buds small (up to 0.125 inch long), set on a small platform and appressed to the twig, with four imbricate bud scales.

Bark: Smooth and gray when very young, developing wart-like corky outgrowths when greater than 3 inches in diameter. Bark often has a splotchy appearance.

Fruits: A small pea-sized drupe (up to 0.375 inch across), dark purple to nearly black when mature, containing a single large seed. Fruits mature in the fall and sometimes persist into winter.

Similar species in winter: None.

WINGED ELM
Ulmaceae
Ulmus alata

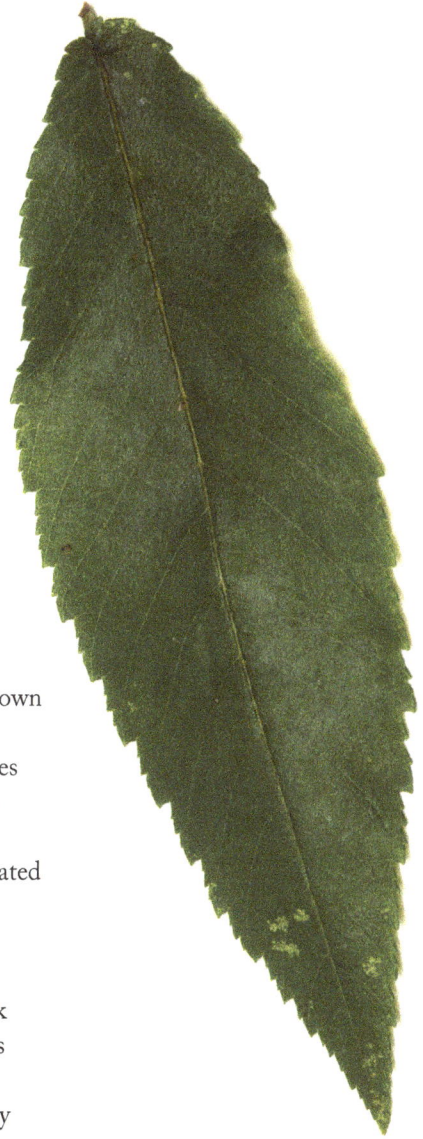

GENERAL DESCRIPTION

A medium-sized tree, up to 70 feet tall, with a broad, open crown and often with ascending branches. Commonly found across the Piedmont and mountains, particularly on drier upland sites and in old fields and along fencerows. Simple alternate leaves are elliptical in shape, rarely more than 3 inches long, with a narrowly pointed tip, an asymmetrical base, and a doubly serrated margin.

WINTER ID FEATURES

Twig and leaf scars: Very slender, slightly zigzag, and dark reddish-brown in color, and usually glabrous. Older twigs and branches typically form broad (up to 0.5 inch wide) corky wings on each side. Leaf scars half circular to nearly circular.

Buds: Terminal buds are absent; lateral buds are narrow, pointed, and covered with dark reddish-brown imbricate bud scales.

Bark: Light brown to dull gray, scaly, and very soft (can be easily scratched with a fingernail). Larger trees sometimes develop deep fissures.

Fruits: A flat elliptical samara, up to 0.375 inch across, with ciliate hairs on the margin and a V-shaped notch on one side. Fruits mature in early spring and do not persist into winter.

Similar species in winter: Slippery elm (page 186) and sweetgum (page 120).

SLIPPERY ELM

Ulmaceae
Ulmus rubra

GENERAL DESCRIPTION

A medium-sized tree, up to 80 feet tall, with an open, irregular crown. Found sporadically across the Piedmont and mountains, primarily in fertile, moist sites and sites with limestone bedrock. Simple and alternate leaves are elliptical in shape, generally broader toward the tip, up to 6 inches long, with a doubly serrated margin, asymmetrical base, and a very scabrous upper surface.

WINTER ID FEATURES

Twig and leaf scars: Fairly slender, slightly zigzag, grayish-brown in color, and pubescent. Exudes a mucilaginous, aloe-like sap when chewed. Leaf scars nearly circular, with visible bundle scars within.

Buds: Terminal buds are absent; lateral buds are dark brown, with imbricate bud scales covered with dense reddish-brown pubescence.

Bark: Similar to winged elm, but often develops shallow, hickory-like interlacing ridges with age.

Fruits: A flattened samara, similar to winged elm but larger (up to 0.75 inch across) and lacking pubescence on the margin.

Similar species in winter: Winged elm (page 184).

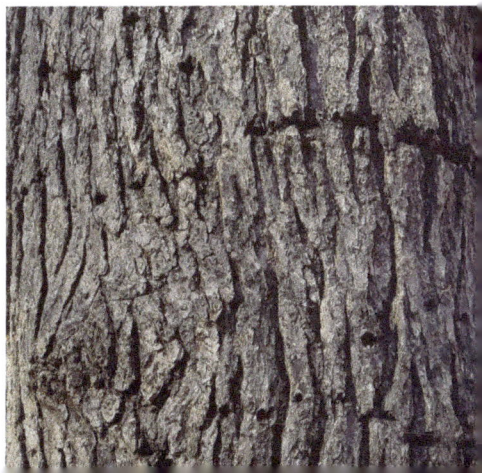

GLOSSARY OF KEY TERMS

ALTERNATE—One per node. Typically used in reference to leaves or leaf scars.

APPRESSED—Pressed close to or flat against another organ, as in a bud against a twig.

BEAKED—Having a narrow, prolonged, and sometimes hooked tip.

BERRY—A fleshy fruit with many seeds.

BUNDLE SCAR—Scar on a twig, within the leaf scar, left by the vascular bundles (xylem and phloem) when the leaf falls.

CAPSULE—A dry fruit that splits open when mature to release the seeds.

CATKINS—A cluster of (usually) tiny apetalous (no petals) flowers, often cylindrical in shape and drooping.

CILLIATE—Having row of short hairs along the margin.

COMPOUND LEAF—A leaf consisting of multiple leaf blades (leaflets). Some leaves are palmately compound (all leaflets originate from a common point), or pinnately compound (featherlike, with leaflets usually oppositely arranged along the rachis).

DRUPE—A fleshy fruit, typically with a single stone-like seed.

EMBEDDED/SUBMERGED—Bud sunken within the leaf scar; often invisible, or nearly so.

EPICORMIC—A twig or branch originating from buds under the bark of the trunk or branch.

GLABROUS—Smooth and without hair.

GLAUCOUS—Covered with a whitish or bluish waxy coating.

INTERNODE—The space on the twig between two nodes.

IMBRICATE—Bud scales overlapping, like tiles or shingles on a roof.

LEGUME—A dry, pod-like, often papery fruit that usually splits along two sides, releasing the seeds.

LUSTROUS—Glossy or shiny, usually smooth.

NAKED—Lacking bud scales

NUT—A hard, dry, indehiscent (nonsplitting) fruit, usually containing a single seed.

NUTLET—A small nut.

OPPOSITE—Two per node. Typically used in reference to leaves or leaf scars.

PRICKLE—A sharp-pointed outgrowth of the epidermis or bark.

PUBESCENCE—Hairiness; short, soft hairs.

PUBESCENT—With pubescence.

SAMARA—A dry, indehiscent (nonsplitting) winged fruit. Some samaras have two wings.

SIMPLE LEAF—A leaf consisting of a single leaf blade.

STALK—The supporting structure of an organ (e.g., a bud), usually narrow in diameter than the organ.

STIPULAR SPINE—Stiff, slender, sharp pointed structure, usually found in pairs, for some species, on either side of the leaf scar.

TARDILY DECIDUOUS—Refers to deciduous trees that retain their senesced (dead) leaves into winter.

THORN—A modified stem, usually stiff and woody, terminating in a sharp point.

TOMENTOSE—With tomentum.

TOMENTUM—A covering of short, soft, matted, or tangled woolly hairs.

VALVATE—Having bud scales (usually two, sometimes three) that touch edge to edge along their entire length, without overlapping.

WHORLED—Three or more per node. Typically used in reference to leaves or leaf scars.

INDEX

ABOUT THE AUTHORS

DONALD L. HAGAN is an assistant professor in the Department of Forestry and Environmental Conservation at Clemson University, where he teaches courses in Dendrology, Forest Ecology, and Forest Communities, among others. He also oversees the Forest Ecology and Fire Science Lab at Clemson, and he and his students conduct applied forest ecology research—largely focused on fire and invasive species in the southern Appalachians and Piedmont. He has authored or coauthored articles in journals such as Forest Ecology and Management, Fire Ecology, International Journal of Wildland Fire, and Invasive Plant Science and Management. He and his wife, Thea, live in Clemson, South Carolina, with their two children, Aster and Lawton.

CRYSTAL STRICKLAND has a Bachelor of Science in Wildlife and Fisheries Biology from Clemson University. She is continuing her education and working toward her Master of Science in Forest Resources at Clemson under the advisement of Dr. Donald Hagan. Her research emphasis is on invasive plant species on the forest floor and how they spread through recreational use. In the future, she hopes to pursue a path in environmental education to help bridge the gap between science and the general public. Crystal's pursuit for a higher education is supported by her husband, Ray, and two children, Brielle and Isaac.

HAILEY MALONE graduated with a Bachelor of Science in Wildlife and Fisheries Biology from Clemson University in 2019. She hopes to continue to combine her passions for illustration and the outdoors as she pursues a career in wildlife biology. She is currently working on another book project, a conservation-themed coloring book focusing on rare and unique wildlife of South Carolina.

ACKNOWLEDGMENTS

Students in Dr. Hagan's dendrology course at Clemson University were the primary motivation for this book, and they provided valuable feedback on early drafts. Aster Hagan (age 4) enthusiastically assisted with twig collection, even when it meant getting her favorite "sparkle shoes" a little muddy. Additional support came from the Clemson Experiment Station, under Project Number SC-170051.

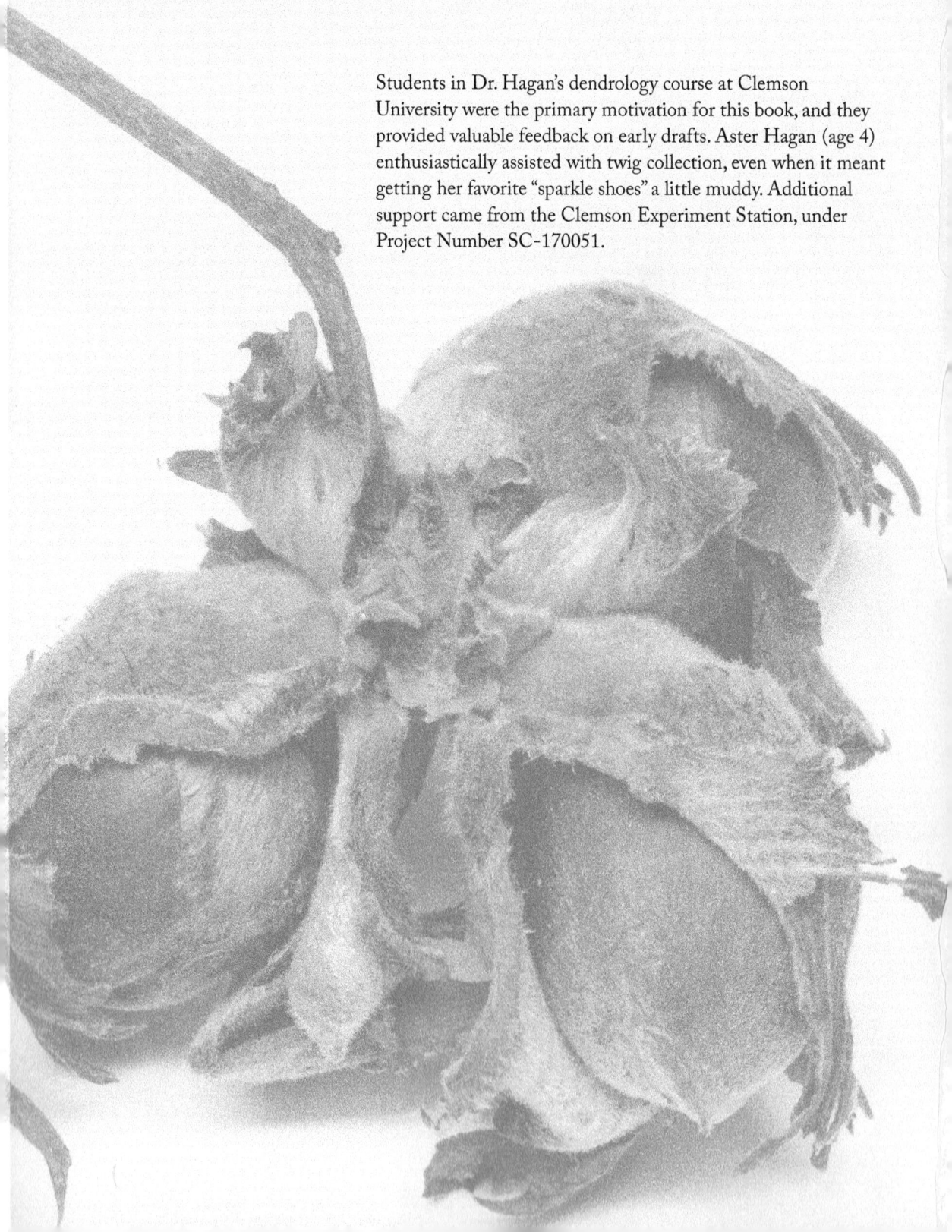

www.ingramcontent.com/pod-product-compliance
Lightning Source LLC
Chambersburg PA
CBHW061217270326
41926CB00028B/4676